CW01665464

It is my intention with this book to welcome everyone who wants to disrupt and enrich their lives – through love and laughter – whether as individual human beings or entire businesses

From Fear to Love

'My My My!
I just passed by to say Hi!'
Life was knocking on my door
I wasn't sure

I thought: 'I just have to survive'
Suppressing my longing to come fully alive
Overwhelmed by fear I found myself getting stuck
For me there wasn't even a starting block

That was, until I discovered love
Not for romance, but as a mindset set to solve
I decided to pause, and take a deep breath
Slowly starting to take a distance to the daily death

Would I dare to lose my foothold for a while?
To dare to live a new lifestyle
Could daring and caring be part of me?
Was that really who I was meant to be?

To choose courage over convenience
And commitment over cautiousness?
My heart being open and expanding
I was used to fear being so demanding

They say any change starts with you ...
Hmmm, I guess that is true for me, too?

KAREN TOBIASEN

The Heart Revolution®

Transform Your Life, Transform Your Business

By Karen Tobiasen

A Profound and Practical Guide to
Personal and Business Transformation

The views and opinions expressed in this book are those of the author. All people mentioned in case studies have been used with permissions and have had names, genders, industries and personal details altered to protect client confidentiality and privacy. Any resemblance to persons living or dead is purely coincidental. All uncited quotations in this book are by the author.

ISBN 978-87-972401-2-0

Front cover image and book design by Artist:
Kathrine Højris (kh@ilovemytype.com)

Published by Nordic Press, Denmark
Printed in Denmark
First printing edition 2020.

Contents

Dedication

My father was the first person to show me the limitations of fear and the opportunities of love. His stage and exam fright, which he was never supported in dealing with, meant he only received an education late in his life. Despite being smart and talented, he walked through life only leveraging a fraction of his capacity as – unfortunately – many of us do. He knew that he did not spread his wings fully and chose to encourage his three children to live a life full of ambition, aspiration and fulfilment – challenging ourselves to the edge of our capacity.

My father first was a farmer and later worked in a factory. He was always full of ideas about how his company could improve. However, as I grew up, I saw how many of his ideas and solutions never materialized because his workplaces did not know how to leverage this capacity coming from the shop floor.

I thought – from an early age – how this was a terrible waste for my father and for the companies. I knew, from that moment, that I wanted to work in the intersection of human and business transformation and potential.

After a long work week, my dad channelled his creativity and inspiration into writing poems, songs, speeches and stories, which he loved. I watched him sitting in his chair on Sundays absorbed in his writing, truly enjoying himself. Similar to how I sit nowadays. He gave me my first inspiration for this book.

The Heart Revolution

Change happens in business and in life. Today's success is achieved by learning how to thrive and come alive – manifesting our deeper purpose and true potential – through transformation.

For that to happen we have to shift our mindsets to build and sustain our own capacity to transform. By replacing fear with love. Waste with value. By enriching our personal and professional lives with deeper meaning and expanded capacity.

This book invites you to step out of your comfort zone, tear down your internal blockers, and follow the Ten Steps of Transformation, for a greater impact in your life, organization and society.

Join The Heart Revolution

TM

Foreword

Earlier in my professional life in the late 1900s, I had the opportunity to experience the power of a strong company culture, as a Partner at Goldman Sachs. We operated as one company working in cohesion and alignment guided by clear ethical principles. It was a formidable experience and we were proud of where we worked. We hired for culture. We fired for culture. It was a culture that was unbeatable and it set us apart. It was a culture created and maintained by the people working for Goldman Sachs worldwide.

In 2015, when I became the CEO of Nordea – the largest Nordic bank with 30.000 people – the Panama Papers crisis hit us and I knew we needed to change our culture. We needed to become the bank that our customers, society, people in the company, their families and, frankly, even my mother would trust and be proud of. During my career in banking, I had seen enough egotistical and self-centered bankers. As a company, I knew we needed to take responsibility for our role in the financial system and the wider society we were a part of. The industry was faced with increased regulations because we had not taken this role seriously enough before.

For us to rise above this challenge, we needed to lead ourselves, each other, and the industry in a different way. We had to realize how we were all leaders. It was not about who we reported to, instead it was about each person's contribution and progress towards the company's collective purpose. It was a move from an ego-centered to an eco-centered culture and it was an absolute must. It was during this period and in meeting this challenge that I met and knew I needed to bring Karen Tobiasen onboard, to work side-by-side with me to drive this important business transformation.

I had already experienced my fair share of failed organizational transformations. Those that failed because they were simply technical exercises; where they did not win the minds and hearts of the people involved, which caused the transformation to stall. I needed myself and everyone else to understand that if we - as the people of the organization - were not transforming, then the company would not transform either.

Change is inevitable. It is the only constant aspect and therefore our capacity to learn and change is our biggest asset as human beings. The speed of this process is of the essence. Technology sets the pace for how fast we have to adapt. Often, setting it exponentially, a concept we cannot fully grasp as human beings. The world has never been more volatile, uncertain, complex and ambiguous, and we need to learn to see this as an opportunity. If we don't our competitors will.

The cultural transformation journey Karen helped us embark on was one of the proudest periods of my career. Working intensively with the mindset of every person within our bank - equally focusing on the frontline team members as well as the top of the business - always with the aim of creating a single, powerful and united company culture. We started the journey by establishing a new purpose, which represented our contribution beyond the walls of our own bank. Throughout the process, we listened to and co-created that purpose with thousands of people in the bank.

This work was new and exciting territory for me. I was encouraged to see how our purpose unified leadership, employees and our community at large. Our purpose and values guided our culture. We chose to change the Why and the How to truly integrate and align with the What and that made all the difference to the depth and speed of the bank's transformation.

The cultural transformation was my responsibility as the CEO, but it was not my expertise. I wanted a clear roadmap and proven approach that allowed everyone to feel engaged and take ownership for the year-long journey.

The process set out in Karen's first book, **The Heart Revolution**, does exactly that. It provides a step-by-step guide for everyone. Karen's words and energy demonstrate how we can all improve our working and personal life and through it that of our businesses. It reveals with clarity that wherever we sit in the organization, we all have an important role to play, every day.

To me, the ultimate power of this book and the process it shares is that it speaks the same language to those people on the front line of an organization, as it does to those in its board room. One voice, one approach, one set of practices. It makes us understand how we serve the same goal much larger than profit.

The Heart Revolution radiates Karen's expertise in the field of human and business transformations. You can immediately sense the depth of research and theoretical knowledge behind the Ten Steps of Transformation, which are provided without being flashy, remaining an accessible and compelling read throughout.

One moment in this book that will always be special to me, is where Karen introduces the Prisoner, Tourist and Player who live in us all of us. I vividly remember how that made me feel the first time I, as an experienced leader, was introduced to these archetypes, presented by Karen at one of our leadership gatherings. It was fantastic to realize, together with 300 senior business leaders, that we all had work to do on ourselves, and to all share a good laugh about it.

I have had the privilege of being the CEO of a large company, but as Karen says in her book: "We are all perfect CEOs of our own lives" and are invited to lead it accordingly. **The Heart Revolution** holds the potential to help us, not only to become better colleagues and leaders, but also, better sons and daughters, brothers and sisters, partners, friends, or simply better human beings. Wherever we are in our lives, it has something to offer all of us.

I trust you enjoy transformation as much as I do. It is here to stay.

Casper von Koskull
Former CEO of Nordea, Global leader, Board Professional

A book for all of us

Dear reader, dear human being,

Never has the world changed as fast as it does now, and never will it be as slow again. This invites all of us to lean into our own personal transformation as well as the business transformation we are part of. We all need to build the capacity to transform – so transformation does not scare us, but rather enriches us profoundly.

This book is for those of us who want to get more out of our private and professional lives and the lives of our companies. We achieve a successful business transformation when we enable it through human transformation.

Wherever you operate in an organization, you matter – regardless of whether your organization is small, big, local, global, private, public, profit, non-profit or civil society.

As individuals, leaders and transformers we come together as one community. Effective business transformations are not designed by an exclusive or elitist few. They are co-created with all of us – people – being part of and inspiring the transformation as an united force.

I am not neglecting the responsibility the leadership of a company has for creating the right conditions. Yet, we are privileged to become part of transformational journeys and when we do, we are obliged to start by transforming ourselves. A company takes no actions, people do.

Collectively, we are our organizations. When they suffer, we will suffer. When we thrive, they will thrive. The same holds true for society. When we as humans and business thrive, so will society.

Warmest

PART I

Gain Your Transformational Foundation

What's Love Got to Do with It?

'And now here is my secret, a very simple secret: It is only with the heart that one can see rightly; what is essential is invisible to the eye'

ANTOINE DE SAINT-EXUPÉRY [1]

From coconut to avocado

'It is good that you have your blazer on', Rosa greeted me. Right away, she knew I didn't get it. She planted a seed right there. Her body was tiny, yet she was filling the space. I was fully dressed in a blazer, entering her cozy psychotherapy environment for the first time. There were crystals and poems everywhere and all I remember thinking was, 'I don't understand half of it'.

I had gladly immersed myself into a master's degree in Gestalt Therapy - an existential/experiential form of psychotherapy which emphasizes personal responsibility and working with the present moment. I wanted to further understand myself and other human beings[2].

Having therapy myself was part of my studies. While in that first hour I didn't actively reject her attempts to get to know me, I had no idea how to fully let her in. She asked questions I had never thought about. The chair felt both comfortable and not. I wanted to stay, and I wanted to go.

The 'me' who was in that therapy room was the high-performing, insecure overachiever studying Gestalt Therapy in parallel with a - more than - fulltime job as a successful executive in a senior leadership position within human resources and transformation for a multinational division. I had just turned 40, lived on a beautiful hill in Switzerland, ate life in big hungry bites, and yet instinctively I knew that there was more to life. I was privileged to be part of probably the highest-performing team I had ever met – headed by an extraordinary human being and business-savvy leader who led and lived by one core sentence: 'We are more than the sum of our parts'. This leader, Mason, deeply believed in humility, collaboration and teamwork. He inspired me from the day I met him.

He was walking down a hallway at a business conference in Frankfurt surrounded by many people that wanted to talk with him. He was in his late forties, tall, athletic, blue-eyed. He was smiling and having fun. I remember thinking, 'He could be running for president'.

I was heading the other way when someone introduced us to each other. Mason stopped and met me with absolute undivided attention when he looked into my eyes while he shook my hand for the first time. I was impressed. Oh, if only I could meet people like that every day – leaving an everlasting impression of comfort and safety with my 'Hello'.

Mason later invited me to attend a strategy workshop in New York, where he wanted to see how I would fit into his extraordinary team. We went running in the morning, worked during the day and socialized in the evening. Flying home three days later full of warmth, inspiration and adrenalin, I was happy and humbled to have been onboarded to my new role with passion and intensity while having 'passed the test'.

I became part of a team that, for several years in a row, won all the internal awards for best region, best customer engagement and best employee engagement. A winning team. The secret to success was no secret: flawless execution delivered with the guiding and gluing principle 'We are more than the sum of the parts' putting the team in the center, not the individual. Mason celebrated when we were ambitious on behalf of the organization and our purpose. He shone the light on personal humility combined with professionalism.

One day I came to him with what I later realized was an intention to brag about what I had achieved. He saw right through it and gently, yet firmly, made me reflect by simply asking, 'That's great, and who did you achieve it together with?' and 'Who and what contributed to this success?' In that moment, without judging me, he helped me see 'my' achievements through a lens of 'we'. He was right. We rarely - if ever - achieve anything great alone! Wow, did I listen to and learn from him, as I always felt his good intentions for my growth.

One evening, when we were all together in a Swiss chalet celebrating another fantastic year, Mason focused his attention on me. 'What exactly are you studying during your Gestalt education?' 'Oh no!' I instinctively reacted. Even though I was well into my own therapy process, I was living two unintegrated lives: one in which I was focused on the outer dimensions of my life, being a high-powered prosperous businesswoman in the fast lane, and a private one in which I was delving deeper into holistic thinking my inner dimensions and conditions.

During my Gestalt studies, I was discovering my inner self, where most cells in my body were screaming at me: 'You are not good enough', 'You need to step it up', 'You are on your own', 'You don't belong'. I had so little self-acceptance that I did not dare to share myself with others, imperfect as I was. Not fully worthy of belonging to this team - vulnerability and authenticity did not feel like an option. Instead, I put on my armor to protect myself from relying on other people, not risking being disappointed.

It all felt predictable and safe. Living parallel lives was, however, draining my energy. From the outside - and by our usual standards - I was living a full life and was highly successful. And yet ... I did not feel fulfilled and didn't dare share and integrate practices I enjoyed in my private life and through my Gestalt studies with my work.

Mason asking this question felt genuine. It gave me the opportunity to take my first cautious step toward integrating the two sides. 'I am studying a psychotherapy focusing on wholeness,' I guardedly answered, 'integrating body, soul and mind.' I felt uncomfortable sharing, afraid of being judged, seen as soft or weird. I had not yet found rational stories and interpretations for my experiences at my Gestalt Therapy studies and how to translate them into a predominately logical world.

'That sounds very interesting!' he enthused. 'What does it actually mean?' I paused, hesitant to share any further, and thought to myself: Is he interested? Should I really share? Mason curiously listened to my answers that evening. Slowly, in micro-steps, I dared to share more of my whole self with him and the team.

It was crazy for me to experience that the more I shared my imperfection in this high-performing team, the more they enjoyed working with me. It was a revelation to me that I was okay, even if I was not perfect. As I connected to myself, I could connect with them. As I saw myself, I could see them. After I had lowered my shoulders some more, I became less defensive and my ability to collaborate and solve together grew.

Life was good! I was on a great path to becoming my more integrated self. Sadly, at that time the world became scarier for me because Mason became seriously ill and quickly had to leave his role. I never got the chance to say a proper goodbye. He left before I fully understood how privileged I had been to meet him. Mason did eventually fully recover and I had the privilege to reconnect with him later in life and continue our dialogues.

Two years into my Gestalt studies and my personal integration journey, our next leader arrived with guns blazing and started firing people. He was smart, funny, fast – with what seemed to be quite different values and a different approach to Mason. Several people I was devoted to left and were replaced with the new leader's previous colleagues.

A new tone was established and, from my perspective, the magic vanished in six short months. We were now also struggling in the business. Whereas I had been close with Mason, my new boss was not working closely with me.

I sensed he had talks with his new team members that I wanted to be part of. I did not feel qualified, relevant and that I belonged. It was clear to me that I would be the next person in the firing line. Fear kicked in and I did not recognize myself.

My output and contribution deteriorated drastically. I became cautious, played it safe and did not speak up. I avoided attention and became a fraction of myself. I loved my job and was afraid of losing it. Or rather, I loved how I had contributed, grown and enjoyed before my new boss arrived. I did not like what I and we together had become. I missed Mason's leadership style and I was yearning for the past.

It took six months to mobilize my courage to ask my new boss's secretary for a meeting with him, too afraid to ask him directly. 'Sit down,' he commanded as I entered his large corner office. Nervously, I obeyed. I was shaky and anxious and had prepared how to courageously express myself without judging him while showing up authentically.

'I am wondering whether you know that I want you to be successful in your role.' I stuttered. 'I know I am not doing a good job. I sense how afraid I am of you and that I might lose my job – a job that I love. I am wondering if you also want me to succeed in my role?'

It was out. I had said it. I felt raw and vulnerable, yet at peace. He looked at me, surprised. 'Are you afraid of me?'

He was quiet for a moment and then amazed me by saying, 'But I am afraid of you!' I was stunned.

'What ... me?' In fact, I had not spent much time reflecting on how I could be perceived by him or anyone else in the organization, not understanding how I could also activate fear in other people. I was tall, blonde, fast, self-confident, accomplished and part of a very successful team. Obviously, I was always wearing heels and a chic blazer. A pretty scary power woman!

This was the first time we genuinely saw each other as human beings, both vulnerable and connected in our fear. It became the start of a potent working relationship – we put our guns back into our belts, teamed up and focused on how we could reduce fear in the organization.

The declining business turned around; we slowly but surely got back on track. Although it was scary showing vulnerability and sharing my fear, it was worthwhile. I never imagined that we would partner up and evolve as human beings as a result of it.

That was the last time I wore heels and a blazer. My therapist was right in referring to my blazer as my shield, my crutch. The change of clothes was a physical manifestation of what was going on inside me. I am a human being with human flaws and flowering features.

The upset with my new boss helped me shift from being a coconut: hard on the outside with an empty core – to an avocado: soft on the outside, yet with a strong core. A movement through a mindset of fear to a mindset of love. Together we turned this upset into a learning process for both of us.

I will forever remember how my output, productivity, engagement, contribution and overall performance improved significantly now I was once again feeling safe and that I belonged.

It would be easy to judge my new leader, but there was no reason for that. Firstly, working for him gave me one of my biggest moments of learning and shift in working life, and I would not be the human being and business leader I am today without that experience. Secondly, we can only change ourselves. When I showed up authentically, he could do the same. Thirdly, we as his team created an insecure foundation when he started in his role. We were all silently grieving Mason's departure, wanting him back. Did we give our new boss a fair chance? No.

In this courageous conversation we had, we met as human beings. Through a different lens, our challenge became an opportunity. My inner journey was the important first step in realizing that if something was going to happen, I had to initiate it. I had to own how I was operating.

When I changed my mindset, our relationship changed. When I felt safe, I was significantly higher performing, whereas when my fear kicked in, I became a fraction of myself. I was too afraid to make any big and bold business interventions. Instead I played it safe, wasting my own and my company's capacity.

I learned that creating safety as a leader is a foundation for peak performance, something I occasionally still need to remind myself, being intense, ambitious and a fast mover. I left my blazer behind many years ago and yet still have to be mindful to avoid mentally putting it back on.

And, oh, what a difference it makes! From a mindset of fear, I generate waste. From a mindset of love ... I generate value.

This is the very essence of this book.

What do you recognize from my experiences in yourself or other people?

All we want is love

Do you ever feel that that life is something you need to survive - rather than to come fully alive? Are you ever more exhausted than excited?

Early in my life and career, while working as a nurse, I had the privilege to support patients who were at risk of losing their lives. I have seen old people dying with regrets and young people dying with grace. It made an everlasting impact on me. It is less the length of your life that matters, but rather how you live it.

Death gives the ultimate perspective to life. Not for us to fear, but to understand what good fortune it is to be alive. Seeing death as a perspective to life has formed how I view and interact with the world. We are all privileged to have been given time on this beautiful planet. Life is short. Life is precious. How can we each live life to its fullest?

My dream is that this book will offer what you need to come fully alive both privately and professionally – to reduce waste and enhance value in your life and your business.

As human beings, we have two overall mindsets from which we can operate: one of fear and one of love. A mindset of fear is one of limitation, protection, scarcity, separation and exclusiveness. It leads also to waste. We want to survive. A mindset of love is one of enough, openness, abundance, integration and inclusion. It creates value. We want to come alive.

Fear contracts, love expands. Fear diminishes, love enriches. Fear exhausts, love excites.

'Hold on!' you might say. 'What's love got to do with it? Love is for family and friends, not firms!'

That is a limiting belief. Love is much more than romantic love. Love is a force for good – in all lives, including business lives. It is our heartfelt commitment to be at our best and to do what is best for the totality. It is our commitment to ourselves, our organization, our community, our planet. Love is way beyond feelings. It is a way of being, a way of doing. It is a choice. It is constant practice. It is the reason why we are here. The essence of who we are.

In fact, love is all we want.

Let's test that idea ...

Can you think of anything you want from a company that is not, in essence, love?

'Yes,' you might answer. 'I only want my pay-check!'

Then I will ask, 'Is that really true?'

As people, we want our company to show us love. We want it to provide us with safety and a sense of belonging and self-worth so we can enjoy, grow and contribute. All this making workplaces great for human flourishing.

As customers, we want companies to listen and care deeply for our needs and passionately develop products that help us improve our lives.

As societies, we want companies to show love and care for the communities we are part of. We want them to show citizenship, helping the community to prosper and having a purpose beyond making money.

No one is in the market to buy fear! And yet it permeates a large part of business and society today. It has been part of how we work for so long that we might not even notice it any more. When we take a deep breath and pause, we know that fear is preventing us from reaching our real potential as human beings, as businesses and as a society in terms of life expectancy and quality of life.

When we instead are in the market for love, we understand that this life is not a zero-sum game whereby if you gain, I lose. We expand together – doing well by doing good – as human beings, as business professionals and as citizens. Human transformation enables business transformation and that enables social transformation. Isn't that the value chain you want your kids and loved ones to aspire to and become part of?

You might ask yourself, 'How do I do well by doing good?

You do it in big and small ways. When you bring a loving mindset. When you are open, honest, partnering up, stepping into being empowered and feeling accountable, when you speak your truth, when you solve rather than suffer. The list of love-based behaviors you experience at work is long!

You might not even recognize when you are fearful. We all are – consciously or unconsciously. When you are in mindset of fear you protect yourself, you are cautious, you play it safe, limit yourself. You might judge other people who are different. You might take advantage of other people for your own benefits, including customers and partners. The list of fear-based behaviors is long. It is human, but not helpful.

Doing well and doing good are not contradicting but reinforcing forces.

Can you sense what a difference our mindset can make to us as human beings, businesses and societies?

When we firmly invite love into our lives and 'love to go business' we enter The Heart Revolution. And now is a good time.

A burning platform: our time, our world

The Fourth Industrial Revolution is in full swing. This technology-enabled revolution is disrupting and enriching our lives at an ever-increasing speed. Robotics, artificial intelligence, biotechnology and the Internet of Things are changing our lives and work significantly. The pace of change is largely determined by technological advancements often happening exponentially. Enormous productivity gains are possible for all individuals and institutions able to adapt quickly to the new reality.

Additionally, we are impacted globally by regulations, climate crisis and pandemics. Expectations, challenges and opportunities for human beings, businesses and societies will never be the same again.

Most, if not all, industries are undergoing significant disruptions. New business and operating models are swiftly emerging, differentiating companies from their peers more than their products and services. Challenges for one company today become opportunities tomorrow for another.

We have known it for a while: The world is becoming increasingly volatile, uncertain, complex and ambiguous.

This requires new organizations, skills and mindsets. If you and I don't transform, others will be more relevant than us tomorrow.

'We need to transform!' human beings and businesses call out. Everyone *knows* that we need to do it ... and we all *want* to do it ... without fully knowing what *it* is.

For years, we have been constantly changing.

As humans we have gone through several industrial revolutions, transforming our societies and way of living in significant ways, often enabling us to achieve higher levels of productivity, performance, welfare and enrichment.

We have worked on eliminating wasteful processes since the early 1900s. We have been adjusting our operating models and how we bring value to our customers since the 1960s. We have been optimizing our value chains - our set of activities that allow us to deliver valuable products - since the 1980s. We been reengineering business processes and optimizing workflows since the 1990s.

We have achieved enormous productivity gains by removing much waste from our companies through these different approaches, making things better and constantly seeking to gain efficiency. Yet we are struggling with transforming and making things different.

We are left with two problems:

1. The majority of all business transformations fade or fail. Companies today live shorter and shorter. Companies do not exactly know what to do differently - this time - to succeed[3].

2. Change and transformation is taking its toll on us human beings - the global workforce. Only 15 percent of us are fully dialed up for the big and bold work required from us. We're living longer and longer, but these days we're more exhausted than excited[4].

These two problems have the same root cause: We underestimate the human dimension of business transformation.

We have invested billions in leadership development, but when asked we prefer different leaders. We have not focused on, invested in and found the keys to the human transformation: Optimizing our inner operating model, our inner value chains.

Today's companies are, from my experience, faced with 30-40 percent waste in terms of human capacity – individual and collective waste in terms of focus, effort, time, energy, agility and execution. This leads to lack of unlocked potential and impact as well as fewer sustainable solutions. Intangible, invisible significant waste.

Fear is the creator of waste! With our fear-based mindset we see the world as a zero-sum game: one of win-lose. We automatically separate ourselves and protect 'ours', leading to wasteful either/or and often polarized choices:

As people with a fear mindset we typically choose:

- To remain with a company even when we are disengaged and resentful
- To stay safe, working harder, resisting new ways to learn and expand
- To protect our own results, rejecting the impact we together can create

As leaders with a fear mindset we typically choose:

- To optimize for our own team: defending my team, my budget – sub-optimizing the totality
- To rely on what we know, resisting the unknown and alternative perspectives
- To drive focused execution, missing the opportunity of flexible expansion

As a company with a fear mindset we typically choose:

- To push for profit serving shareholders rather than all stakeholders and the greater good
- To focus on business transformation, missing out on the human transformation
- To trade short-term performance for long-term performance and transformation.

Do you recognize the waste created by a mindset of fear - also in your own life?

Companies get stuck, slide, slow down or stop in their transformations because of resentment, resistance or rejections of their people - often without knowing it. I guess we have all experienced culture eating strategy for breakfast. Not pretty.

There is no business transformation without a human transformation

The Fourth Industrial Revolution will only accelerate this picture. When we view through our lens of fear, there is much to be anxious about. However, there is another way.

Unleash value - stepping through fear to love

When we instead view the same situation through the lens of love, we understand that we are in the market for love. We understand that life and business is not a zero-sum game. It is not a burning platform. Instead, we tap into our burning desire to grow together by doing good as human beings, as a business and as a society. We become more resourceful than exhausted.

'Hold on,' you might say. 'What's love got to do with it?'

My answer is: 'Pretty much everything.'

With a loving mindset, we step into ownership of our transformation. And, as we only create value and no waste, we optimize, we partner up, we innovate, we co-create, we find solutions, we constantly evolve and we adapt, all while staying relevant. We get excited.

From a mindset of love, we learn to operate as bold and brave transformers - exactly what both The Heart Revolution and the Fourth Industrial Revolution require. To turn today's challenges into tomorrow's opportunities, we need to humanize businesses. When we as humans transform, our businesses will transform.

Love leaves no waste, only value.

Building your Transformational Capacity

You might say, 'I know I need to change, and I want to - but how?'

Building our Transformational Capacity as individuals, teams and organizations means facing our fears and embracing another way. Transformational Capacity enables you to not only resourcefully respond to what might come your way, but more importantly to shape your own future, lead the way in unknown surroundings, remain relevant and continue with the journey, even when the road ahead is blurry and bumpy.

When we change our inner operating model from fear to love, we access our almost infinite capacity to grow. When we optimize our inner value chain, we create a strong collaboration between our head, hands and heart, leaving no waste.

You will build your Transformational Capacity through the Ten Steps of Transformation.

You might ask, 'Is it that simple?'

Simple, yes! But not easy.

You are probably used to studying biology or technology, but less so studying yourself and how you think, feel and make sense of the world. In this School of Transformation, you will build your Transformation Capacity through self-discovery of your meaning: the Why of your life – along with your mindset: the How of your life – impacting how you manifest: the What of your life.

There are three essential questions for you to find answers to:

1. How can you ignite and align yourself towards **a greater meaning?**
2. How can you turn challenges into opportunities through a **loving mindset?**
3. How can you elevate your **impact** as constant **manifestation?**

This book will help you to find the answers. It offers many more questions inviting you to reflect and actively find your answers and your way. Transformation is an ongoing journey, where you never arrive, but rather constantly evolve, developing your agility, which is your ticket to both The Heart Revolution and The Fourth Industrial Revolution.

In a profound and practical way, you learn a new way of listening, learning and acting. You will tap into your immense capacity to enjoy, grow and contribute, to the benefit of both yourself and your business.

Don't be shy to focus on you. This is the only place a real transformation can start. Here, you will always be the driver, never the passenger. There is never a dull moment on the journey, even though you are often invited to slow down to speed up. Transformation is like tennis: You never get really good at it unless you practice.

If that is what you want, this is a good place to be.

When you and I leave the vicious circle of fear, which focuses on separation, and enter the virtuous circle of love, we can integrate and create win-win-win solutions for everyone. This means that we strive to bring value in each interaction, including how we relate to projects, people, problems, prospects and the planet – leaving everyone and everything, including ourselves, better off than before the interaction.

This is what I am longing for. What are you longing for?

Transforming together

Like never before, this book brings love fully and uniquely into our business world, to our workplaces. It ignites your curiosity and challenges you to understand fear and love in new and profound ways. It is also a spiritual book, providing you with inspiration for how to live life fully, bringing what you and I know to be true into everyday life in businesses. It is an existentialist book, as all transformations are existentialist, dealing with how we as human beings and businesses exist in the world.

None of us have to wait for our leader, our CEO or the transformation office. This is an invitation to all of us to be empowered, to do something great for ourselves, our teams and our companies. You will have the toolbox you need within this book. The collective actions of all of us working for an organization in different roles – from board to front line – determine the destiny of our organization. Together, we are the organization. Together, we are the society.

May this book ... inspire you ... puzzle you ... disrupt you ... evolve you ... and enrich you. One step at a time, no matter how small or big, but always towards better.

Enjoy Your Heart Revolution

The Waste of Fear and the Value of Love

'Fear and Love can never be experienced at the same time. It is always our choice as to which of these emotions we want.'

GERALD G. JAMPOLSKY [5]

Before diving into the Ten Steps, I invite you to zoom out to look at the big theme of this book: Fear and Love. To know and be aware of the difference between love and fear – including how you personally experience love and fear and how they impact your output and your surroundings – is a privilege. It provides you with freedom.

We live in a world of duality where we know something by what it is not. As we have light, we have darkness. As we have peace, we have war. As we have love, we have fear. Fear puts love into perspective and vice versa. They co-exist, and we alternate, back and forth, from a mindset of fear to a mindset of love.

We choose our mindset in each moment, sometimes consciously – and often unconsciously. We are never both in a mindset of fear and love at the same time since our brain cannot cope with being fearful and loving simultaneously.

We are in a constant dance with love and fear throughout our lives. The choice we make between love and fear defines how we live our lives. It's probably the most important choice we will ever make. Love and fear are opposites, but not equals. As familiar as fear might feel, you and I were not born to be motivated by fear, but rather to explore and live love.

The impact of fear

The purpose of fear is survival. It stops us from walking into oncoming traffic, stepping off roof tops and carelessly handling poisonous snakes. In the course of human evolution, the people who feared the right things survived to pass on their genes and the trait of fear perpetuated our species.

Fear can be many different things, including fear of failure, fear of public speaking, fear of losing, fear of the unknown, fear of success and also fear of love. Fear can show up as frustration, anger, shame, blame, exclusiveness, self-protection, self-centeredness, helplessness, manipulation and more.

Do you recognize those parts in yourself as fear?

When you choose a mindset of fear, you immediately impact your physical, emotional, mental and spiritual capacity. These four dimensions of you are interdependent, inseparable and interconnected as a system. When one part changes, the rest changes.

The physical impact of fear

Fear starts in our brain and spreads through our body, making remarkable adjustments for the best defense reaction. Our reptilian brain, called the amygdala, is first alerted. This almond-shaped caveman brain calls the shots for the rest of the body whenever we perceive a threat, be that a predator, a car, a dangerous cliff, our boss or a stage.

The amygdala pushes us into fight, flight or freeze mode, shutting down large parts of our more mature brain and creating absolute focus on the perceived threat. The stress hormones cortisol and adrenaline flood our body. We become hyper-alert. In only a few seconds our body is ready to tackle the danger head on. Thank you, Amygdala!

Our reptilian brain is highly reliable and has helped us survive as a species. At the same time, it is also rigid, impulsive and compulsive, influencing our behavior unconsciously. This incredible response is absolutely needed when we are in real danger and was especially helpful for our ancestors, whose next-door neighbor might have been a saber-toothed tiger.

It is less helpful in our modern reality, where we face fewer real dangers and yet we remain programmed to respond with the same full-blown bodily reactions when receiving our boss's feedback or trying something new.

When fear takes control and becomes a more permanent resident it is unhealthy and has negative consequences for our whole body. We can become exhausted with stress, burnout and potential illness. Our brain capacity and our ability to learn are significantly reduced.

Do you recognize what happens in your body when you are in fear?

Despite the negative consequences, fear also brings an adrenaline and dopamine rush. Many of us can become highly addicted to it, taking on tasks too big – working harder than is good for us and yet loving it as we feel alive, teetering on the edge of our abilities and testing our limits, which all feels dangerously exciting!

Fear impacts your physical capacity in a sensational and lifesaving way in the short term and in a dreadful and life-destroying way when you more permanently visit the field of fear. This diminishes your overall impact and output.

The emotional impact of fear

Fear impacts our emotional or relational capacity since behind each of our fears lie our basic human needs, including our sense of safety, belonging and self-worth. We bond emotionally and connect when these needs are met. Our ancestors met many of their basic needs when they gathered in tribes, sometimes being violent towards other tribes while protecting their own tribe.

Today we continue to gather in tribes, including our work teams, company, friends, school mates and families. We feel positive emotions towards them, and they make us feel safe and that we belong. When we are inside our tribe, other people become outsiders to us. Maybe we see them as strangers, competitors, enemies or simply as other people. Who is in your tribe?

Our emotional capacity is significantly impacted from a place of fear. We protect ourselves in the realm of 'me-myself-I', rather than contributing to other people. We divide and simplify our world into 'us' and 'them'. Our listening and sensing skills are neither practiced nor developed and we might lack emotional control. Our ability to relate with other people and build strong relationships and partnerships can suffer.

Having a competitor who is seen as the absolute enemy can drive the effort and execution of power for a company. Nothing feels better than beating the competitor, creating an emotional bonding in the tribe – the company – so strong that it prevents people joining the competitor.

Internally, the same behavior leads to silos and hierarchies, internal fights, creation of win-lose situations, camouflage of failures, politics, sub-optimization, sandbagging and much more. These are wasteful challenges that many companies are struggling to overcome. Do you recognize them? How are you adding to the struggles?

The mental impact of fear

Mentally, fear heightens our senses, creating intense focus and helping us stay on our toes. The fear of failing can make us raise our bar, creating a strong output – at least in the short term, but often exhausting us in the longer run. With a mindset of fear, we will often make simpler decisions, seeing options as good or bad, right or wrong; many of us find this calming. Fear-based decisions and actions often result in short-term benefits since we stay within our comfort zone.

The flip side of focus created by fear is the tunnel perspective that comes with it. It reduces your ability to solve more complex problems creatively. Mentally, you contract rather than expand and you lose the bigger perspective. Do you recognize yourself in that tunnel - where your capacity is significantly reduced? We are all there from time to time - and it is not a nice place to be.

In a business context a fear-based mindset can make us determined, decisive, dominant and directive. This gives us a sense of safety for a while since we feel we know what to do and where to go.

As we lack the ability to see the bigger perspective also as a business, we do not solve complex challenges easily, if at all. Instead we hone in on incremental changes, trying to make things better rather than different. We feel stuck in some areas. 'We have tried this before', people call out, but we try again, now a little harder.

The spiritual impact of fear

When we are busy with fear, there is limited space available to connect to our spiritual capacity. Our human spirit, our soul, our consciousness, our human experience. The short-term focus on our needs easily sacrifices the growth of ourselves. 'What's in it for me?' we ask. We have difficulties serving something bigger than ourselves, which will fulfill us in the long run.

In a business context, a mindset of fear means that we are likely to be predominately focused on earning more money, serving immediate shareholders. Do you know companies with this limited focus? Are you working for one right now?

The value of fear

Fear helps us to stay alive, sometimes helping us stay one step ahead. Insecurity, our desire to belong and being good enough, can be an enormous driver for achieving great things. It drives us to set ambitious targets, overachieving to feel safe and to belong.

Many people, including myself, have made it far in our careers fueled by our fear, consciously or unconsciously dealing with self-doubt like: 'Am I safe?', 'Will I belong?', 'Am I good enough?' – often pushing that fear further onto our organizations.

Fear helps us identify our unmet needs. Fear might have protected and served us up until now. Yet, it is unlikely to take us to where we want to go. We need another way now.

The waste of fear

When we react out of fear, we respond automatically with our caveman brain. Sometimes we get it right and sometimes it only addresses a short-term fix that ends up causing more problems down the road. From a mindset of fear, we typically do not plan ahead; we are in our reactive mode, where we choose safety before purpose, making us inconsistent at best.

Fear absorbs much productive energy from an organization. We become stuck playing it safe, protecting and promoting ourselves and not focusing on the aspects that move the business forward.

When we fear our colleagues, we become political, we fight internally and we derail our focus partly or completely from the tasks at hand, harming our company's performance. When we choose short-term before long-term gains, when we choose to stay quiet and safe, it increases the risk of mistakes and – most importantly – of repeating them. When we don't speak about our mistakes, we will not learn from them. When we work in fear, we are less capable of learning as an organization. We are less innovative, less creative. Fear always leaves waste. Do you?

'No passion so effectively robs the mind of all its powers of acting and reasoning as fear' Edmund Burke says. When we hold a mindset of fear, we firmly believe in limitations - that life and business are zero-sum games - and therefore tradeoffs are inevitable. For example, protecting the short term before the long term, protecting me before you and protecting the company before the rest of society.

Our brain contracts, our worldview contracts. Profit, at the expense of purpose, people and planet. In fact, when you stay cautious and play it safe, you are less safe than ever. You become reactive to what happens to you. You stay put - while the world moves.

The cost of fear was not very clear for me before I experienced how I had a fraction of my normal capacity with a significantly reduced output for the period during which I was afraid of my new boss. Imagine this scaled to 100, 1.000, 10.000 or 100.000 people. The waste of fear is enormous and often we do not even notice.

Do you recognize the waste associated with fear in your life?

The impact of Love

When you look at a newborn, you know that love is our natural state when we strip ourselves from our ego and fear. Love is our essence.

We are designed and wired to connect. In a neural ballet, we connect to other people around us constantly [6].

Whereas homo sapiens physically are weak as a species, we have survived because we are a highly social species: interconnected, interdependent and interpersonal, with our superior mental, emotional and spiritual capacity.

We have managed to catapult ourselves to the top of all species because of our awareness and our consciousness. We support each other, stay together, leverage and appreciate each other's complementary competencies and capacities.

The physical impact of love

When we embrace a loving mindset, our body is positively impacted since our cortisol levels decrease. Unlike adrenaline and dopamine, oxytocin has no adverse side effect other than being highly addictive.

It establishes bonding, trust and social affiliation between human beings. The strongest example is the love between a mother and her child. Oxytocin reduces anxiety and drives a positive mindset.

A fear mindset activates one neurological pathway through the activation of the amygdala. Positive emotions activate the brain through the more evolved part of the brain running our executive functions. This evolved part of the brain focuses our attention; predicts consequences of our actions; allows us to anticipate events in the environment; controls our impulses and emotional reactions; plans for the future and coordinates and adjusts multifaceted behaviors like problem solving and complex decisions while learning from them [7].

When we connect to our hearts, we improve our physical, emotional and mental capacity, including better sleep; feeling calm; having less anxiety; being less fatigued and less depressed between 24-56 percent [8].

Isn't that surprising? This means you become stronger with more capacity.

In a business context, when you activate your loving mindset you activate more capacity to do business without becoming exhausted. Your output enhances in volume and staying power.

The emotional impact of love

Our emotional and relational capacity is impacted by a mindset of love since we activate our ability to step into the positive qualities of passion, compassion, ownership, collaboration, courage, selflessness, risk-taking humility, integrity, honesty, vision, self-awareness, purposefulness, intuition, wisdom, generosity and gratitude.

Phew! These are big words for many of us that we might aspire to live more fully. Can you see how these qualities can expand and enrich you?

The impact of gratitude was a small revolution to me when I realized that my brain cannot cope with both being angry and grateful at the same time. When I genuinely say 'Thank you', my brain shifts to a loving mindset. The same is true for you.

Studies have shown heart patients can improve their heart condition by writing a daily gratitude journal listing three things they are grateful for, for eight weeks in a row. Several of their heart markers showed positive signs. A grateful heart is a healthier heart! When was the last time you genuinely thanked someone? Your heart loves it when you do [9].

With a loving mindset, you also take care of your basic needs, safety, belonging and self-esteem. When you do that you can release the brakes that keep you from achieving what is truly possible [10].

In a business context, activating your loving mindset means activating a positive outlook, motivation and engagement. As you feel good, you bond, you trust and you bring additional value as you collaborate and depend on others, leveraging your complementarity, becoming more than the sum of your parts. Exactly as Mason showed me and my colleagues.

The mental impact of love

We have, until recently, thought that IQ was the most important driver for achievement and performance, but recent studies show that our attitude matters as much as our IQ when it comes to learning and achieving [11]. A positive and loving mindset simply takes us further as it expands our mental capacity by up to 30 percent. Think about it - 30 percent! What a life hack! [12]

A positive mindset opens our mind's eye to options all around and allows us to take in multiple perspectives without becoming defensive. An open heart creates an open mind. We might believe we only have one brain. In fact, we have three.

Our head brain has 86 billion neurons, our gut brain has 100.000 billion neurons, and our heart brain 39 billion neurons. Our heart is the biggest electric magnetic field in the body and sends as many messages to the head brain as it receives.

Our three brains are great together and make far better decisions than when we only use our head brain [13].

Are you connected and using all your three brains? Do you sense the difference it makes?

As we expand our mental capacity, we can solve problems that from a fear-based mindset were insolvable. We become creative and curious. We become solution oriented. We are able to mentally take a wider view seeing the situation from multiple perspectives and listen to people with different voices.

While fear reduces our ability to learn, the opposite happens when we feel safe. We are prone to engage in ways that create learning: sharing with other people, asking for help and experimenting [14]. Optimal learning and growth happen when we stand on the border of what feels safe for us, tip-toeing outside our comfort zone. How do you best learn?

New requirements from society, regulators or customers will force businesses to choose a more responsible approach. Embracing a loving mindset means making decisions that are beneficial for multiple, if not all, stakeholders. The main value creation happens through better decisions and solutions.

The spiritual impact of love

When we step into a loving mindset, we see opportunities more than problems. When we combine what we love doing - our passion - with how it matters to other people - our purpose - we can significantly outperform ourselves and everyone else, while also enjoying ourselves.

When we understand that we, in essence, are love. We understand the unlimited potentiality we are and will continue to explore.

When we activate our spiritual capacity, we see abundance rather than limitations and we can move from an ego-focused 'I-win-you-lose-perspective' to an eco-focus 'win-win-win-perspective', which not only is possible but more sustainable [(15)].

Do you recognize when you are holding a win-lose perspective?

In the business context, we now understand the consequences of our actions and are able to integrate both the short- and long-term and thereby create solutions that take future generations into consideration, as well. We connect to the bigger 'Why' of things.

Are you connected to the bigger 'Why' of your work and your organization?

When we as individuals and companies understand that we are society, and that society is not different to us, we are likely to seek for the optimal set-up where we do good and do well at the same time. Our world becomes one of much less 'either/or', and much more one of 'both/and'. We become inclusive and integrating. Are you?

The myths of love

Just as oxytocin does not have any recorded negative side effects, neither does love. It might be the myths of love that make us fear love, or the excuses we make for not fully embracing love.

Love – a sign of weakness: The first myth of love is that we are – perceived to be – weak when we show our full authentic selves, including the softer, more vulnerable parts. Showing a loving mindset at work and not keeping it only in our private life might be seen as weak or inappropriate.

We believe we are at risk putting ourselves out there in a situation where we might not receive the same level of vulnerability or authenticity back from our colleagues. What if they exploit and prey on us because we show weakness?

Do you recognize these thoughts – feeling that love is risky?

It is a gamble and our hearts are willing to gamble where our head is busy calculating the risks. We fantasize that our vulnerability makes us weak; however, when other people show their vulnerability, they have an enormous impact on us – as they share their ups, and downs, their humanity ... we listen.

As they expose themselves, we find them brave. As they connect to their hearts, we connect to them and we remember them for how they made us feel [16].

Who is remembering you for how you made them feel?

Our brain cannot distinguish between whether or not we are giving or receiving love. It releases oxytocin anyway – with the associated benefits. As you give, you will receive. Love is a non-depleting resource

– the more you use it, the more there is. Love is always around; the question is whether you have the courage to live it?

Love – a sign of softness: The second myth is that a loving mindset is one of peace, love and harmony, giving love the reputation of being soft and fluffy, which it is not. True love is to give, and to do what is needed in any situation, which means you take the totality picture into consideration.

Sometimes, this means that the loving thing to do – the right thing to do – can be seen as tough or hard. For example, this could be letting a lower-performing person go from a job because the person is likely to do a better job in another situation and the company is better off having a more suitable person in the role.

Love does not prevent consequence management. In fact, it is managing consequences, which means to hold all of us and each other to account as to what we have agreed. Many organizations and transformations are struggling with taking the necessary consequences because we feel uncomfortable. We want to be liked by people or choose for short-term convenience.

Recognizable?

Yet, managing the necessary consequences is a loving act, serving all parties, the system and the direction set for the totality. When you are not taking the necessary consequences, you are putting the totality and the flow of the transformation at risk. When you care, you dare.

The business value of love

From the previous sections you have gained an understanding of what love can do for you, and what you can do with love, including what value love brings and the value you can create with love for yourself and for other people. The value of a company these days predominately lies in the value of its people. We are our companies. We are our organizations.

This also means that our organizations are dependent on us building our Transformational Capacity. What happens when we all dress up in love and bring our hearts to work? What happens when the whole organization operates from a loving mindset?

Love as a life and business enabler

With our loving mindset we listen, learn and act in a new way where we deal well with dilemmas, uncertainty, complexity, tension and pace – our world today. This mindset helps us, as individuals and as companies, to find the right balance and integration between our business performance where we focus on the What; and our organizational health where we focus on the How; and our social impact where we focus on the Why [17].

When we all courageously integrate and balance short- and long-term goals, transforming while performing, we allow our organizations to flow, flourish and function.

The best companies and their people understand this and create every form of value that matters, including experimental, emotional, social and financial, delivering value to all their stakeholders.

They understand this is the only path to long-term competitive advantage. Do you see the value we can create when human, business and social transformations co-exist, enriching each other and evolving together, acknowledging our full interconnectedness and interdependence?

Love leaves no waste, only value

You can choose love over fear and thereby value over waste. You can choose to make every day one of disruption and enrichment. The biggest hindrance to exploring the land of love might be your fear of love. You might feel vulnerable to 'lose your heart'.

When you pause, connect and reflect you can deepen your awareness and understanding of the choices you have and the impact your choices have on your current and future life, as well as on your colleagues, organization, family and friends.

How much power do you want fear to have in your life?

Your mindset determines the choices you make, and you become the choices you make – choices that have soft or significant implications. We have seen how fear and love have a different impact on physical, emotional, mental and spiritual capacity. Love leaves no waste.

Value creation can come from fear and love, yet love is a much bigger human and business value generator than fear. Simply put, 'Love is more!'

Are you looking for more fear in your life? No one is! Love is what we, as human beings, want to experience and explore while we are here. You are not here to survive – but to come alive.

Love is a choice: a bold, daring, caring and absolutely worthwhile one.

PART II

Transform Your Life

Illustration of the Ten Steps of Transformation®

For your orientation as you travel through the Ten Steps of Transformation.

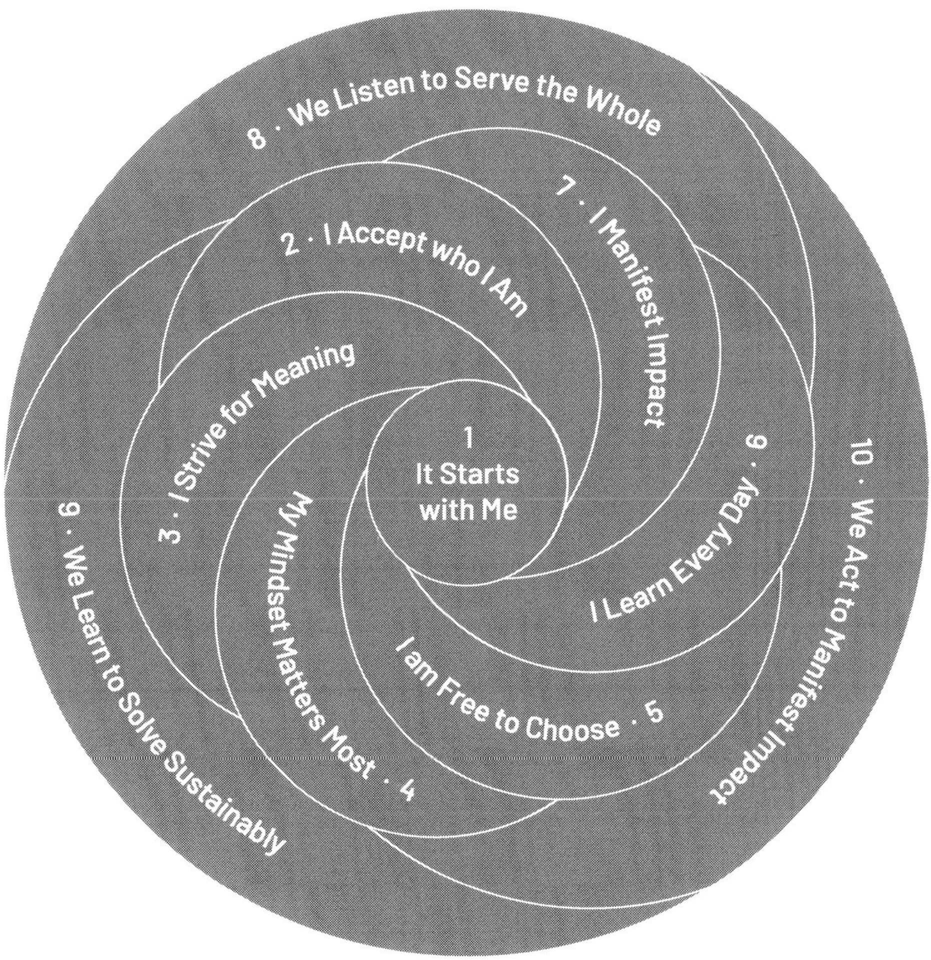

Welcome to the Ten Steps of Transformation

Many of us speak about transformation. We want it, we need it ... but what is it?

My definition of transformation is: 'A radical change that sets a new direction, doing things differently – creating another level of output. It is a change in appearance, character and perspective. All transformations require change, but not all change is transformational. Transformation means there is no way back. It is a continuous and never-ending journey.'

A profound and practical journey

The Ten Steps capture the essence of what enables a true transformation in you, your work and your organization. They take you full circle, from building insights and meaning into making conscious choices around your mindset for you to impactfully manifest.

The first seven steps equip and evolve you as a human being and to own that for yourself. These are the foundation for steps eight to ten where you, together with your colleagues, will contribute to creating more effective business transformations.

You are not separated from your organization, not it from you or from the rest of society. We are all part of this eco-system: connected, interdependent, interlinked. When we learn to transform individually, business will follow suit. Similarly, if we don't, then neither will our business nor the world around us.

For each step I share my personal and other people's stories inviting you to reflect on yours with love and laughter. You get the Why, What, and How of the step, as well as profound and simple practical Signature Practices for you to adopt and apply daily, assisting you to move from a field of fear and waste to the land of love and value. A concrete toolbox to inspire you to start with yourself. Even when you are deeply inspired by the Ten Steps of Transformation, they will only work when you practice them again and again and again.

Have you read books before that gave you insight but then you never took it further? That would be a big mistake with this book, wasting your time – and dare I say – your potential.

Be playful. Take one step at a time: flirt with it, get to know it, fall in love with it. And then live it – at your own pace. The Ten Steps are not linear steps, but building blocks towards a higher level of awareness, choices and actions.

Some steps might feel more effortless than others; some might have you feeling you'll never get there. Feeling stuck reveals a great potential. You might revisit a step multiple times – yet, you will never be the same when you return – as you are constantly learning and evolving.

There are at least three ways to accelerate and anchor your learning in relation to this book and thereby your Transformational Capacity.

First, invest in an awesome notebook and make it your transformation journal. Throughout the book I invite you to pause, connect and reflect on important transformational questions. Don't miss them.

Secondly, find a transformation buddy – a friend, colleague or partner – to team up with during the process of implementing the practices.

Thirdly, I recommend you join The Heart Revolution community that can support you with all the tools and practice to continue to assess, build and sustain your Transformational Capacity. For more details see the section 'Welcome to The Heart Revolution' at the end of the book.

You might feel that you slow down, whereas in fact it will speed you up. You will expand your Transformational Capacity through three key pillars: meaning, mindset and manifestation. They accelerate your transformation and make it sustain. Three pillars relevant to all of us as individuals, and collectively as organizations and society.

Before you dive into how you build your Transformational Capacity through the Ten Steps of Transformation, let's look at the context and lives of our companies and why they need us to build our Transformational Capacity.

It is time to step into real ownership for the current and future wellbeing of your company or organization.

Greater meaning: expand your capacity to listen to and serve multiple stakeholders

Companies today are met with fast-growing and fast-moving expectations from consumers, citizens and society. We want companies to consciously serve all their stakeholders, guided by a higher purpose, balancing people, planet and profit - not as a marketing strategy, but making a real positive and visible social impact.

As exciting as these expectations are, they also make life for an organization much more complex, multi-facetted and challenging with many dilemmas, choices and problems to unfold and solve. Many businesses are struggling to find their feet and are under time pressure to adapt to this new reality.

It is easy to look at a company as an entity outside ourselves, perhaps becoming upset about the fact that companies are not becoming purpose-led and values-guided as fast as we want them to. But who is a company if not you, if not me? When we are at our best, our organization will be at its best. The big question is now, how do we get there - fast?

Together, we need to create organizations and cultures with an expanded capacity to listen to and serve multiple stakeholders. Many of us - and our companies - don't have this expanded capacity today because most of us are not fully engaged. That is a problem and opportunity for both us and the companies we are working for. How is your engagement these days - really?

Leaders think they are doing a good job; however, the majority of employees would rather forego a pay raise to have their leaders fired. Billions of dollars are spent on leadership development, yet it does not prevent us from having a significant waste of talent, human capacity, levels of contribution and commitment. That is a problem and an opportunity for us [18].

Do you know what waste you create when you are leading?

Many of us are longing to work for truly, purpose-led and values-guided companies. The bad news is that although they exist, they are few. The good news is that we are the ones who can change that situation. When you and I consistently choose to bring our hearts to work, we build loving, listening, compassionate communities, cultures and companies.

Sounds soft? Look at the facts: These organizations are better collaborators, more trusting, more inspired, more committed and have lower turnover. As people feel valued, they have an increased sense of dignity and pride and they build positive emotions, have less anxiety, and recover quicker from illness [19].

Wouldn't you want to work for such an organization? Wouldn't you want to co-create such an organization?

Imagine stepping fully into a greater meaning. Imagine you stop spending any time and effort on defending, protecting and promoting yourself. Freeing yourself from tiring activities! Instead you choose to step up and step in - bringing your voluntary effort into the mix, doing not what you have to do, but what you want to do [20].

When you are at your best and are pulled by your company's as well as your own purpose, you move from a perspective of 'me' to 'we', allowing you to listen deeply to understand how you best can serve, inspire and engage your multiple stakeholders also beyond your company walls. As our interconnectedness with the rest of society improves, we often understand the root cause of our challenges much better [15].

When we, as people in a company, tap into the energy of why we exist, our greater meaning as a company, including our role in society, we understand the importance of building a fair exchange with all our stakeholders. We want attention, energy, ideas, solutions, products and value to flow effortlessly between all parties involved in creating what the company offers to the world. When we do that, we create win-win-win solutions where the overall size of the pie enhances - and no one loses out.

These companies and their people are recognized for their greater meaning and their expanded capacity to listen to and serve multiple stakeholders - for example, Ikea with its People and Planet Positive Plan taking a solid stand on sourcing raw material for products responsibly, or Whole Foods being at the forefront of food consciousness, creating a market for natural, healthy food [(21)].

As you build your Transformational Capacity you are ready to bring yourself and your organization to join the club of companies that are pulled by purpose.

Loving mindset:
boost your capacity to turn challenges into opportunities

Listening to understand our stakeholders is an absolutely necessity for us to flow. For a company to also flourish, we need to combine listening with a new way of learning to solve.

Many companies shorten their life expectancy because they don't know how to solve their many new and complex problems, trying to solve them with their old tools and approaches and working hard incrementally to improve their situation.

We risk being stuck in linear business plans, key performance indicators, reviews facilitated by leaders and colleagues who know best. For example, Kodak did not foresee the impact of digital cameras, Blockbuster did not acknowledge the convenience of internet streamed movies and Nokia did not accept the power of smartphones.

Linear plans and incremental improvements make us feel safe, but we risk being bypassed by exponential movers such as Amazon making things different.

Imagine fully stepping into a loving mindset. To assess and solve your and your company's toughest challenges - those that keep you and your colleagues awake at night - you need to be willing to let go of the old beliefs and mindsets that have served you so far and instead embrace a new mindset and approach relevant for your current challenges. Be open to reinvent yourself again and again to allow your company to continue to flourish [22].

Consider that you only help your company to flourish when you learn to constantly grow, adapt, renew and reinvent yourself. You secure the long-term health of your organization by staying relevant. This requires that you learn to be comfortable with uncertainty, new perspectives and tension. Walking the bumpy and blurry road of transformation requires stamina, courage and patience from all of us.

In fact, your learning agility will, to a large extent, determine how fast your company will evolve. Instead of protecting yourself, you have to leave your comfort zone or make the mature choice that this is not a path for you and therefore gracefully find another place to contribute. Do you recognize that you also have a choice to say: 'this is not for me'?

When we step into a loving mindset, we help ourselves as well as our company because we access up to 30 percent more brain capacity. Yes, 30 percent more! [12]

This allows us to solve more complex problems with increased speed. When we let go of being afraid of not knowing and approach challenges with more curiosity and openness, we will see the opportunities that exist. The challenges that keep us awake at night are complex and can therefore, typically not be solved on our own. We need multiple perspectives; we need to collaborate, to partner up.

When we are pulled by partnerships we can see further, adapt faster and co-create farther. In that way, we will turn today's challenges into tomorrow's opportunities - leading the way. Our collective effort of holding a loving mindset will help us to create a culture where we also learn from what is difficult, what includes dilemmas and what is complex. As we step into courage, we are willing to hold the tension of that also.

Imagine yourself in this place - where you are able to sense and serve what is needed now. This requires that you acknowledge the past without judgment. It requires that you calibrate and accept the present without cynicism.

When you do that you can start co-creating the future. When we all meet in that place, we all have a place from where we can eliminate the waste tied up in resentment, resistance and rejections.

Can you sense the power of that?

When we all stay relevant as human beings we build and sustain companies that flourish. These companies are recognized for their loving mindset and their accelerated capacity to solve complex challenges together and ahead of the competition again and again and again. Look at the success of Google, which has built a culture that attacks problems not people.

As you build your Transformational Capacity you are ready to bring yourself and your organization to join the club of companies that are pulled by the power of partnership.

Impactful manifestation: mobilize yourself and your colleagues, raising your impact

Several companies manage to learn to listen to understand. They also learn to solve and, yet, they are struggling to stay the course in their actions and day-to-day functioning, including mobilizing their full organization to raise the impact through their actions.

With the Fourth Industrial Revolution in full swing, the world is changing so fast that old ways of working and operating are no longer valid. Solutions of yesterday do not fit tomorrow. Companies are living shorter and shorter lives these days as they have difficulties to run their businesses while transforming them at the same time.

To protect short term, we often hold back the company's pace of change, and as our company evolves slower than the rest, it will be left behind. Alternatively, we focus too much on transforming, leaving our business performance without enough intensity and attention.

We are at high risk of returning to old behaviors and mindsets, getting stuck in the transformation because we don't manage to mobilize all of us – the whole organization – for sustainable impact.

This requires that we bring our Why: fueled by a greater meaning, and our How: fueled by a loving mindset into our actions into our What. Our Why and How need to guide and lead our What in a forceful and consistent way.

Imagine you fully stepping into impactful manifestation. You are not relying on the ranks to resolve; rather, you lean in and take your role seriously as an interconnected individual taking ownership for your institution.

Your organization will function optimally when you remove barriers for focused execution including your own resentment, resistance and rejections that might be standing in the way for progress and change. You lead the way as you stay consistent with what has been agreed and courageously call out when you and your colleagues are deviating for good and less good reasons and take the needed consequences to always raise your impact.

When you relentlessly eliminate waste and create value every step of the way, you make things better in every moment of every day through constant innovation and experimentation.

How is this for you to imagine?

We constantly improve and evolve our ways of working so they always serve our customers while keeping us happy, healthy and high performing. When we always leave situations and people better than when we found them, everywhere in the organization a new more conscious culture is established – one that we can commit to and be proud of, where we are able to manifest sustainable impact every day and everywhere.

We are pulled by potential, our collective potential. Mobilized in unity, interconnected and linked as a web, as a living organism, collectively removing barriers for execution. When we mobilize our resilience, we build and sustain companies that function. These companies are recognized for ability to mobilize the capacity of all their people to manifest impact.

Look at the success of Toyota, where everyone lives the philosophy of Kaizen – owning the change (kai) for good (zen), driving continuous improvement and change. The whole organization understands that every small step matters, leading to the constant adaptation and evolution of Toyota.

As you build your Transformational Capacity you are ready to bring yourself and your organization to join the club of companies that are pulled by the potential of all their people.

You might now ask: Really, can I have that impact? How do I live this life that holds more potential for me and others?

Walking the Ten Steps of transformation will allow you to do just that.

Enjoy the journey

Step One: It Starts with Me

'We need not wait to see what others do.'

MAHATMA GANDHI [23]

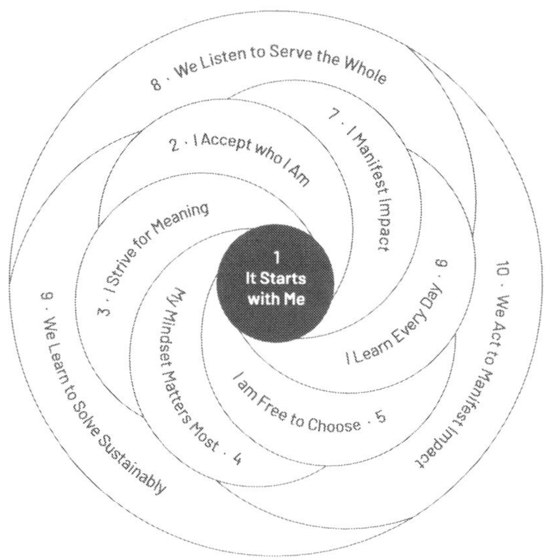

This first step is the most rewarding and also – potentially – the hardest. Stepping into your ownership, authority, authenticity and power to do and create what you want in life. To lean in, to grab it, to be empowered. To fully activate your potential. To become the CEO of your life. Starting now.

You might say to yourself: 'Can I really be the change I want to see in the world?'; 'I am only one of our planet's 7.7 billion people.'; 'Should I lead myself and not wait for my leader?' and 'Does it really matter how I show up. Do I matter?'

Absolutely, yes!

We all have the power to have a significant impact. As the saying goes, 'If you think you are too small to make a difference, try sleeping with a mosquito.'

You matter and make an impact every step of the way – small or big.

While you are waiting for others to lead you and your life, you are wasting your potential. When you change, people around you change. You expand your impact – your positive ripple. Your first change might be to choose to smile at strangers in an elevator and not stare at your phone, to choose to spend the organization's money as if it was your own, to celebrate others when you feel like promoting yourself or caring for your customers' needs rather than their wallet.

These seemingly small steps make a difference to you and to people around you. This is how small gets big. One step towards better, step by step. As soon as you are sloppy and let it slip, you are likely to return to where you started. The more you dare, care and share, the stronger ripple effect you create being the change you want to see at work and in the world.

Smile and the world smiles back at you

How we impact other people we do not fully know, but brain cells called mirror neurons are part of the explanation [24]. These cells fire when we perform an action such as smiling or reaching for a cup, or when we observe someone else performing that same action.

Have you ever been in a meeting where someone yawns? I bet you ended up yawning as well. The mirror neurons collapse the distinction between seeing and doing. Old Louis Armstrong was belting out the truth: 'When you're smiling, the whole world smiles with you'. He drew our attention to the ripple effect through the mirror neurons in his song.

Without mirror neurons we are likely to be blind to the actions, intentions and emotions of other people. When I see you smiling, my mirror neurons for smiling fire up too and I experience immediately and effortlessly – in a milder form – what you are experiencing. They create resonance exactly as a raindrop touches the ocean: the ripple effect. Cool cells indeed!

You might argue: 'I am influenced by my upbringing and surroundings – so how can I change?'

Yes, you are impacted by your context and conditioned by your upbringing, your parents, society, friends and colleagues. Your work is to become aware of how they influence you for you to make a conscious choice as to how much you want to let that happen going forward.

Many of the world's heroes offer you inspiration as to how it can be done. Oprah Winfrey is one of the most recognized, influential and well-respected women in the world. During her childhood she experienced racism, abandonment and sexual abuse. Through her talk shows she has transformed the way we talk about controversial topics like politics, racism and child molestation, creating a safe place for people to share their stories in front of millions of people watching – so we all can learn and feel seen. She has become a famous leader because she dares to be herself. Strong, courageous, caring, loving, sensitive and, above all, a human being – just like the rest of us.

'Yes, but she is very talented', you might challenge. Indeed, she is. Aren't we all?

German physicist Albert Einstein skipped class; his professors did not take him seriously. It was a struggle to find a job before he became a patent clerk. Every day he would sit down and review patents, which had a lot of mathematical equations in then. From his modest patent clerk office in Switzerland he developed his very foundational theoretical work.

He failed a lot. He struggled a lot. He was alone in being convinced that his work was right. Scientists thought Einstein was crazy when he argued that light can bend. His persistence and doggedness kept him going while facing one objection after another – transforming and revolutionizing how we perceive space, time, gravity and light.

Albert Einstein was a master in the field of integration. With his penetrating and original mind, Einstein combined science and consciousness. He spoke universal truth, as a scientist, even when it cannot be measured.

'Yes, but it takes a long time to make an impact', you might continue.

Within 14 months, 16-year-old Swedish Greta Thunberg transformed from a lonely schoolgirl with a handwritten black and white sign striking for the climate outside the Swedish parliament on a Friday in August 2018, to being acknowledged as one of the biggest advocates of the planet by many leaders, stateswomen and men. A remarkable ripple. Her burning desire to impact the planet became positively infectious and she, less than 1.5 years after her first day of strike, organized and engaged four million people in a worldwide climate strike in 161 countries.

'Yeah, but her style is questionable', you might object.

As a change leader, she creates disruption and divides people. Many people follow her because she role models how it can be done. Seeing her making it happen ignites many of us to believe that we too can make a difference.

Many other people resist and judge her approach, her intensity and even aggression, clouding how her message is received. I tip my hat to what she has achieved despite dealing with several mental challenges such as Asperger's Syndrome and selective mutism which for her means she only speaks when necessary. It is so easy to point fingers at people making a difference, wanting them to do it differently.

Who are we to point fingers at people stepping into the arena, daring and caring greatly to change something for the better, when we are comfortably observing them from our cozy chair within our comfort zone? From our comfort zone, with these judging comments - we might discourage others from living their life to the fullest, making an impact.

I don't know about you, but I don't want to be without these and other great leaders who inspire me continuously. Dead or alive, they serve the world every day in a significant way.

Many change leaders did not start by being rich and famous. They took their first brave step being passionate about the topic that was meaningful to them - and one step led to another. We tend to be impressed by their fame, their smarts, their impact, their wealth, their glamour. In reality, what makes these people really impressive is their willingness to persevere, to overcome struggles, to dare and dare enough to share their opinions and continue to do so when people are shaking their heads and looking or walking the other way [(25)].

It is their patience, conviction, care and courage that set them apart. Despite facing adversity, they are determined to make the world a better place - step by step. History is full of examples of a small and thoughtful committed group making big changes in the world. Could anything ever start in a different way?

I know the idea of changing the world can sound so grand, distant and big. And yet all it takes is for you to start changing your own world, noticing how and when you create value for yourself, your team and the people you are serving with your work.

Let's take Caroline. She is 19 years old. She is famous in my life. I have only met her once at a small New Year party. She is a beautiful, sensitive and a spiritual human being and yet loves her life as a soldier. Why? She shared with me how, during military exercises, she marches with her fellow soldiers through an endless amount of cold water and thick mud. Together, they have to carry a heavy stretcher.

She is exhausted and almost giving up when her male colleagues without blame and shame take her turn. In that moment she regains her strength. She and they know that they all give what they can. That makes them united and equal. She experiences self-respect and being respected.

They are euphoric as they finalize the exercise together, dwelling on and celebrating their insights. And this is what she teaches me, with fireworks accompanying her messages in the background:

1. It is not the size of your contribution that matters, but your willingness to contribute when - and with what - you can.
2. The heroes are not the strongest, but those giving all they have to give.
3. Asking for help when needed makes us progress faster together.

That night and still today I am impacted and impressed by her clear wisdom and wish that more senior leaders would listen to the wisdom of her and other young people.

I am grateful for the many people I have met on my journey that have fired up my mirror neurons. People who have taught me by example and excited admiration and emulation. I also realize that people follow me. It is an honor and a responsibility! It makes me reflect even deeper on my own actions. What kind of example do I set every day? How do I act? How do I speak?

Do you know who is following you and for what?

Am I owning it?

We were 18 of us in a cozy attic in a rebuilt farm-house in Denmark - and four hours into our Gestalt foundational program. 'Think about a person who you are annoyed with these days', our Gestalt teacher instructed us.

Immediately, a person came to my mind. A work colleague, who recently had been getting on my nerves. I was spending much time thinking about him and what he did.

'Select three words that describe the characteristics/traits that you do not appreciate with that person ', our teacher continued. I jumped at the task and three traits came easily: unambitious, lack of ownership and honesty. These words described him quite well, I nodded to myself. It was easy to come up with them! It felt so good, so satisfying to pick these words, thinking 'No wonder I am troubled working with him!'

'Now ', the teacher continued instructing, 'please find a partner within the group and share where you recognize the same three characteristics within yourself '.

'What? Me? No way! I am not like that. I am exactly the opposite!' I argued with myself. Looking around at my fellow students I noticed that I was not the only one feeling uncomfortable facing the exercise. The next half-hour we all shared with a co-student how these characteristics were also true for ourselves. One by one, trait by trait. Slowly, but surely.

Unambitious? Well, I recognized an area where I was staying within my comfort zone, playing it safe, and hence not being fully ambitious.

Lack of ownership? Hmmm, I had a project where I was free riding, leaning back and being highly dependent on other people who were pouring energy into the project.

Lack of honesty? Yes, I had not brought my relationship with this colleague to a better place and had not been honest towards him about how I felt. I had even pretended that I was getting on with him – as I did not want him to sense anything – as i feared that he would ask me what was going on. Here, I had been neither honest nor honorable!

Ouch! It took a while and it was not easy to take in. The teacher circulated the room supporting our process, making sure we were not jumping ahead too fast but really digesting and taking back our part. As I took back and owned these three characteristics within myself, my attitude towards my colleague changed.

Gradually, I better understood – and in some parts I started liking – him. After all, he was like me. This was my first confrontation with my own projections, and I understood that they were my natural defense mechanism against impulses or qualities I dislike and do not accept about myself and, therefore, I put them onto other people. This is an advanced blame shifting and shame dumping we all do.

Nothing has ever been the same after I realized that what I judge, I possess! As I grew up with quite a judgmental voice inside me, it is helpful for me to always ask myself the simple question: 'How do I recognize this characteristic, quality or feeling within myself?' And surprise, surprise: In the vast majority of cases, I recognize the part I don't like in others in myself.

When we celebrate, evaluate or point fingers at other people, as I did with my colleague, we create a distance rather than fruitful collaboration. When we are judgmental towards our leaders, team members, customers and partners we destroy value, wasting time and energy. Have you ever seen any progress come from judging anyone or anything?

From this experience I learned that almost anything I think about other people, I can find and relate to in myself. As much as I would like to sometimes get rid of it – I own it. I am not in imprisonment waiting for other people to change. Instead, I lead the way, creating a ripple.
What elements from my experience do you identify with in yourself or other people?

If only ... only if I ...

When I started taking ownership for myself and my behaviors, I started paying attention to my language. I noticed my self-judging language, using words such as maybe, possibly, probably and other tentative words.

I often caught myself starting sentences with 'If only ...' followed by something where I wanted other people or situations to be different. Underlying the statement was typically an explanation or excuse that allowed me to deflect the blame and stay safe, not needing to change anything myself.

For example, 'If only ... they had as much energy as I have!'

I was dreaming about utopia and people being different than they were and exactly how I wanted them to be. I came to realize that my energy could be inspiring as well as intimidating. It was painful to admit that my energy could drain other people's energy. And yet as I learned to moderate my energy level, I experienced energy coming back from other people.

Instead of saying: 'If only ... they had as much energy as I have!' I said: 'Only if I balance my energy, will other people have the space to offer their energy and ideas.'

Yes, that felt different! Actually, quite exciting. Sure, I felt some guilt: 'Oh, I have been taking up space with all my energy!' At the same time, I felt strengthened by now recognizing that I could do something about it. I felt intrigued to try one more – this time a little more profound and difficult.

'If only ... it wasn't always me.'

Truthfully, I didn't come up with this one myself. One day a good colleague almost shouted at me: 'Why are you always insisting on owning everything yourself?' 'What? What do you mean? No one else is stepping in!' Totally worn out, I defended myself, now more exasperated by this annoying interruption. I often felt that I was the only one taking ownership, achieving results. Staying late when other people were leaving. Coming in early before the rest.

I felt nothing would happen if I didn't do it. People were relying on me, I told myself, often feeling lonely and exhausted. A real martyr. By calling me out, this colleague helped me understand that I was the common denominator in the many situations where I was overworking and over-owning. The pattern belonged to me, not to someone else. Thus, I had to also own how to change it.

'Only if I ... ask for help, inviting true collaboration, can other people experience co-ownership.'

As I started turning words around, something changed in and around me. It was the first time I really took charge of my own circumstances and understanding of my working world.

Let me share one last 'If only ...' example. Having vocalized the first two to other people, this one I had never shared. I kept it to myself as part of my inner dialogue because it would have been too much of a taboo sharing.

'If only ... people were as fast and smart as me.'

Ouch. Self-righteous, arrogant, pompous and not easy to face. While processing this, I realized that whereas I love to work with fast and smart people, my greatest fear was to be 'found out' as not being one of them, and thereby being excluded from that tribe.

Whereas I could live with not being the fastest runner, I had significant difficulties not being the fastest thinker and thus feeling small and inadequate. This insecurity was so strongly embedded in me that I overcompensated by judging other people, all of which was distracting me from taking the actions that mattered. How smart was that?

'Only if I ... accept my own limitations will I be able to accept other people.'

The effect was not immediate, but rather little by little. Instead of feeling imprisoned, I felt empowered. I knew that I could do something without waiting for other people to move or change. As my thoughts and approach changed, things in and around me also changed.

They seemed like small changes, yet productivity, engagement and new ideas drove progress for me and my colleagues because of my changes. As I felt empowered, other people could too. We all enjoyed more, embracing our work with more effortless ease. I was inspired and intrigued to continue the journey. I practice 'only if I' on a regular basis – especially when I am under pressure. Noticing my language helps me catch it.

All big changes start small. To change our work and world, we only have to start with one step at a time. One small step – always towards better.

Pause, connect and reflect. How does this step – It Starts with Me – make you think and feel?

Do you have a habit of starting sentences or thoughts with: 'If only ...' expecting things or people to be different, or with: 'Only if I ...' taking full ownership of your impact?

Signature Practice: Own It

It is time to bring out your transformation journal, activating your heart and hands.

Why Own It?

Starting sentences with 'If only' is a natural defense mechanism, indicating that you judge or blame people, places and situations. This is human, when you don't want to or know how to change yourself. Your excuses or explanations at the same time prevent you from changing.

In this way you give yourself permission to stay with old habits within your comfort zone. For example, 'If only we had more products' might be your excuse for not selling. 'If only my boss would give more direction' might be an excuse for you not stepping into self-leadership and owning it.

Although human, it is not helpful. Shifting from 'If only ...' to 'Only if I ...' allows you to achieve all of the following:

- **Take Ownership.** Grow instead of being grumpy.
- **Create Value.** Instead of wasting energy – create value.
- **Connect.** Instead of blaming and judging – connect.
- **Lead.** Invite people to follow you.

How to Own it?

Applying Step One into your daily life: reflect about how you use language. Words give life and form to your reality. By consciously choosing your words, you impact your perception and thereby your reality.

When do you start sentences with 'If only ...' expecting things or people to be different? And when do you start with 'Only if I ...' taking full ownership of your impact in any situation?

- Do you sense the difference?

Write down three relevant examples, where you expect, want or hope people to be different than they are and where you try to delegate a challenge you have by wanting someone else to change. What are your favorite three examples?

Challenge yourself to go further in honesty with yourself, facing also the 'If only...' you are least proud of. In this way, you will gain most benefit out of this practice.

Complete the sentences below with your reality:

- If only ...
- If only ...
- If only ...

Reflect

- What do you think and feel expressing these statements? Uplifted, annoyed, frustrated, big, small or ...?
- What impact do your thoughts and expressions have on you, your way of being, your work and your organization?

Turn these sentences around one by one, starting with 'Only if I ...' followed by how you want to create a better situation. As hard as it can be, I invite you to complete the sentences with what you know to be true about what you can do, not expecting any change from other people.

Complete the sentences with the action you really want to take.

- Only if I ...
- Only if I ...
- Only if I ...

Sense

- What do you think and feel now and has anything changed?

The good and bad news is you own it! It is for you to change and you can. When you change 'If only ...' to 'Only if I ...' you step into leading yourself and your life. You don't have to wait for other people or leaders to lead you – neither in your private life nor your professional life.

The more you practice swapping from 'If only ...' to 'Only if I ...' the easier it becomes until you almost don't think about it any longer. It has become a healthy habit for you to reframe a situation you don't like by starting your sentences or thoughts with 'Only if I ...'

That empowers you right away. You will occasionally revert, especially under pressure. That is human! The only way forward is to practice, practice, practice daily.

Pause, connect and reflect

After using the Own It practice for a period, cement your learnings.

- What waste do you create when you are not 'owning it' that you want to leave behind for the benefit of you, your work and your company?
- What new value do you create when you 'own it' for you, your work, your company?

Moving from 'If only ...' to 'Only if I ...' is an essential mindset shift. As you change, so does your impact.

Only if I focus on love ...

Sarah was a 32-year-old mother of two sons, Thomas, four years and Peter, two years. She was one of my first patients as a newly educated nurse. I first met Sarah in her narrow hospital room right after the doctor told her she had AIDS. The sun was shining, and she looked me in the eyes. Her eyes were blue and very expressive; she was shaken, yet staying calm.

Two years earlier she had given birth to Peter. As the birth was tough and complicated, the doctors chose to give her blood transfusions. Two years went by where she enjoyed her boys and being the family she had always wanted. Then she started repeatedly catching colds from which she could not fully recover.

Already slim, losing weight and finding herself being increasingly fatigued made her go to the doctor. Having AIDS 30 years ago, there was no overall cure, only palliative care to help Sarah with all the side effects. Sarah only lived three months from the day she received her diagnosis.

There could have been many reasons for Sarah to start any sentence with, 'If only ...'. 'If only giving birth hadn't been so difficult' or 'If only the doctors had given me a choice of whether I wanted a blood transfusion to recover faster, I would not have contracted HIV'. Sarah chose not to step into the endless list of 'If only's. Instead, it was clear to her what to do in the few months left. Her beacon was who and what she loved.

Her first relief was her husband receiving his test results. He had not been infected. I witnessed Sarah tapping into gratitude and celebrating that her kids would still have a father.

She knew that her young kids would not remember her as they grew up. She wrote a letter for them to read when they turned 18. A complete love letter, telling them how much they were wanted and longed for.

Her biggest wish was being together with her kids and husband in the last hours of her life. It became a beautiful moment full of tenderness with soft music playing in the background. Sarah died holding her husband's hand, her kids with her in her hospital bed. It is almost 30 years since I said goodbye to Sarah, and she remains with me most days of my life.

Moving from life to death is, along with birth, the biggest transformation we experience during our lifetime. It was an honor to be with and follow Sarah and other patients in their final months and moments. Sarah taught me so much about living, in the midst of dying.

As harsh as this story may feel, Sarah teaches us how transformations can be done without resentment, without rejecting reality as it is - despite it being hugely painful. We learn the essence of grace and dignity and what love can do. She shows us how to live life to the fullest while we have it. She demonstrates that no conversation is too difficult to have and that no 'If only' is ever needed in business or otherwise. What do you learn from Sarah?

The waste of waiting for others

Think about the organizational capacity tied up and wasted in pointing fingers, blaming, dividing and fighting instead of uniting around making progress. The business potential of taking ownership stepping into an 'Only if I ...' mindset at all levels and in all units in an organization is substantial. Starting with you is the first step.

It only takes you and a few inspired focused colleagues to make a real change in your company, removing waste and instead bringing value. For example, 'Only if I really listen to our customers, do we manage to understand what they need '. And, perhaps you are, like me, inspired by Caroline, the soldier who said, 'Only if I contribute with what I can will we solve our current challenges'. 'Only If I ask for help when needed will we make progress fast together'.

Remember to validate your 'Only if I ...'s. Do they bring value to the business when you implement them systematically?

When companies get in trouble, they have typically been waiting too long to initiate their transformation. But who has been waiting? You and me. Why are we waiting? What prevents us from grabbing the opportunity to lead the way, by calling out what is needed to get done?

Fear creates the waste of waiting for someone else to take the lead. I am not neglecting the responsibility of leadership. And yet there is so much we can do whatever our position in the organization.

The waiting puts the company at risk of not getting into the game early, wide and deep enough in the organization. It takes courage - a loving mindset - to step out of playing-it-safe mode and instead take ownership for your own transformation and for your company - as if it was your own.

Step One is the start of acknowledging the tremendous potential you hold, creating a positive impact in relation to customers, colleagues, leaders, partners, families, children and friends.

Always, if you are in doubt or want to accelerate your transformation, say to yourself what you know to be true: *I am the perfect CEO of my life!*

Before we move to the next step, note down your answer to the following question in your transformation journal.

As I dare to dream, what change do I want to be in the world?

Step Two: I Accept who I Am

'Out beyond ideas of wrong doing and right doing there is a field. I'll meet you there.'

RUMI [26]

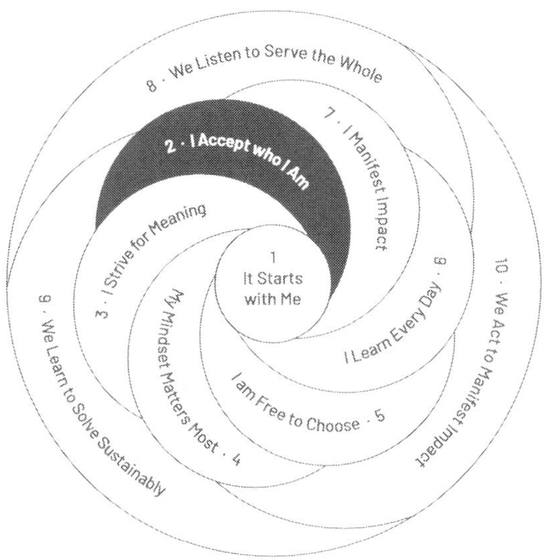

Accepting who you are is the essence of Step Two. You can only change yourself when you fully accept who you are, right now, without judgement; loving yourself as you are. This does not mean accepting all of you at once, but rather one dimension at a time.

When the American novelist and poet Gertrude Stein in 1913 wrote in her poem *Sacred Emily* 'Rose is a rose is a rose is a rose', she inspired me to understand that things are what they are, including you and me, whether you and I like it or not. This is true for you as an individual, for your team and your company.

Only when we stop fighting against who we are and when we stop pretending that we are different, living up to the image people or we have of ourselves, can we start living an authentic life - releasing energy for change. Stress and anxiety exist in the gap between who we are and who we would like to be.

Step Two helps you eliminate the waste of pretending and defending slowing down your transformation as well as your company's. The bigger you perceive the gap in your life to be, the bigger your energy drain and thereby the greater the waste you will experience.

As a company and in a company, we often pretend to be something other than what we are - for example, overselling a product, asking for more budget than is needed or greenwashing our goals or the status of a business.

Let's take greenwashing as a phenomenon. Do you identify with the following?

You report the project to be well underway and in 'green', even though you know it is in reality 'red' because you have challenges with the project. You might not even think about your behavior any longer as you have done it for years.

You might report it 'green' because you hope to turn it 'green' in the coming days, reflecting your dreams rather than your reality. You might color it 'green' because you are afraid of what your boss will say if it is 'red'. You might call it 'green', since this is how your colleagues do it. 'This is how we do things around here' you explain to yourself.

The lack of transparency and honesty hinders you from building trustworthy connections to your surroundings and those around you. It prevents you and the company having the right level of conversations and acting fast on challenges you and the company have.

Imagine this lack of transparency scaled to a whole company and how this behavior and lack of speedy and diligent action can lead to significant challenges and waste for a company.

When you choose to slow down and feel how it is for you, for example, to report it as 'green' when it is 'red', how does it make you feel? In that moment, when you accept who you are – in this example, someone who greenwashes – energy for a real change can be released.

It might also be that you decide to continue to 'greenwash' and then at least you have achieved full transparency towards yourself as to what you do and how you operate. Rose, is a rose, is a rose, is a rose.

Rushed and angry and so ...?

I rushed down the hallway exhausted and digesting the endless number of meetings I had attended earlier that day. My team member was waiting in the small meeting room I entered. The day was grey and cloudy, although I did not pay much attention to anything but the task at hand. Our board presentation had been moved forward and I was worried, having too little time to prepare with the quality I wanted and valued. I felt insecure in my first global leadership role in a global software company, which meant reporting to our executive board on a regular basis.

Tense from the many meetings and the pulled-forward timeline, I did not waste any time on greeting my team member, Logan. Instead, I directly asked him, 'Please show me the presentation for the board'. 'We have not managed to do anything yet, so I have nothing to show you', he murmured. 'But we had a deadline and you promised me. This cannot be!' I exclaimed while punishing him with my now angry eyes. He looked down. Silence!

While I was probably right with my message, I was completely off in my tone and by showing up with so much frustration and anger, and with no desire to connect. My reaction was out of proportion with the issue at hand due to my fear of not delivering good quality and thereby not feeling good enough.

I had not shared with anyone, not even myself, how I felt about the pulled-forward timeline. Instead, I was back in my familiar mantra of: 'Buckle up and let's get it done'. At this time in my career I was still wearing my blazer, and it would take another four years before I would let it go.

I often said to myself, 'If only people would produce what they promised to deliver' and again and again my mindset was confirmed by people not delivering what they had promised, proving – or so I thought – that I could not fully trust people.

Back then I did not curiously explore the root cause of the lack of delivery. Instead, I kept repeating my behavior, kept being frustrated, only to get exactly the same results again and again, different from the value I wanted to create. I was not yet fully trusting myself, so how could I trust Logan or anyone else? I had not realized yet that the only one I could change for change to happen was me.

The outcome of the meeting would most likely have been quite different if Logan and I had checked in with each other first, sharing where we both were. If I had included him in my concerns for the board presentation, my frustration would probably never have escalated to anger.

Equally, he would have shared what was going on for him, allowing me to see him. We would have had a much better chance of finding a path to strong output, offering us an opportunity to pause, connect and reflect, and focus fully on the topic at hand, together.

Instead, the meeting ended right there, while I was feeling angry, creating waste instead of value. When I had cooled down, I felt ashamed. I had shouted at one of my people. That was not okay! And I did not know how to apologize. I felt it would make it worse.

Instead I felt guilty and by not reconnecting with him my guilt and shame grew, tying up conscious and subconscious energy until 15 years later, where I reached out to him to make my amends for my behavior.

This healthy habit of making amends, I wish I had taken on earlier in my life, since I have found it to be so healing for both parties to connect after a painful experience. I thought about all the hours I had wasted thinking about Logan and the impact this experience might have had on him, instead of reaching out and connecting.

Do you recognize this pattern in yourself? Many of us waste our time and energy thinking about what we could or should do or what we could or should have done or not done, rather than accepting who we are and focusing on what we want to do.

Losing my temper was particularly sad and shameful for me after I had worked systematically on abandoning that part of my character. My father had a temper and showed it, living his life with his emotions full on. 'You have your father's temper', people pointed out to me early in my life.

I understood from the tone that it was something I needed to get rid of, something to manage, something not good. I, therefore, viewed it as a big mistake every time I was angry or showed frustration or negative feelings. For a long time, I neglected that side of me.

During my Gestalt Therapy education, I learned how I could sense and share what was going on inside me, including my negative emotions. It was a revelation to experience that when I shared my adverse emotions early on with ownership and without suppressing them, I could better manage, preventing a sudden explosion of emotions.

From my experience with Logan, I learned the importance of understanding what is really going on for me, including accepting who I am. What elements in my experience do you identify with in yourself or other people?

What you resist, persists

Do you sometimes want to be different from who you are today?

Stronger, faster, slower, firmer, harder or softer? Often, we strive for being something other than what we are. Modern technology has fueled the constant stream of images and updates that we can continuously hold ourselves up against and compare ourselves to.

Perhaps your way of coping is to dwell on all the ways in which you could be better. 'If only I was good enough, I could afford what she has'. 'If only I wasn't so lazy and skipped that gym class, I could also look like that in a swimsuit'. Or, perhaps you join me in the club of dealing with painful events or thoughts and emotions inside us by packing them away like I did for 15 years with regard to Logan.

Much energy and thereby waste is tied into 'should, ought, must'. It feels like a long road that never ends.

Change is a paradox. The more we do not want to be who we are, the more we will be that way - exactly like when I did not allow myself to be angry and kept having outbursts. What we resist, persists[27].

Often, when we push for a fast change, nothing happens. You cannot pull the grass to grow. It grows when you water and nurture it. The same is true for change. You need to slow down before you speed up.

You might think, 'But isn't acceptance a passive state - so where will that take me?'

Acceptance is not giving in to your life situation and becoming a passive tourist in your life and in the world; rather, it is for you to become aware and to face your reality and then move into action and change.

Mobilizing your inner detective

Think of yourself as a detective, curious to understand, enhancing your awareness of what is going on in you and in your life. What thoughts are you noticing right now? How do you feel in this moment, sitting here reading? Who are you right now, without adding any judgement of good or bad?

As you practice looking curiously at what is going on inside you, it is rewarding to understand that whereas your thoughts impact you, you are not your thoughts. They serve as important input as to what is going on for you right now. They come and go, like clouds passing in the sky. And the sky (you) stays, even when it is cloudy. Thoughts and feelings are part of you but are not you. Isn't that a relief? You become more and more aware of yourself, of the world around you and how you relate to it.

Feelings give you key input as to what is going on for you right now and what is important for you. Connecting with your feelings is therefore a good way of connecting with yourself. The more you observe and engage with your thoughts and feelings, the more you build your self-awareness and the more emotionally intelligent you become.

You learn to stay attuned to your inner signals, recognizing and observing how your feelings affect you, including your job performance. The more you repress or constrain your feelings, the more you constrain your ability to feel joy, love and freedom as well as other feelings [28].

Can you sense how your self-awareness is the foundation for your transformation?

'Okay, but I am so busy. I don't have time to build my awareness', you might object.

You are right. Most of us are busy, yet making little progress. Research indicates that 47 percent of the time, we are mentally off-task. Our productivity suffers as we multitask, thinking about other things and indulging in our addiction to action. It is a perfect strategy to avoid what is actually going on inside ourselves.

Research suggest that multitasking can reduce productivity by as much as 40 percent. Think about it, 40 percent! [(29)] If it was your company, would you want people to multitask? Would you want yourself to multitask rather than mobilizing your inner detective?

This becomes a vicious cycle. Not being present is a disease of our time caused by all the distractions that now exist. The consequence of this life of multitasking is that we exhaust our brains. We achieve a sense of accomplishment, not realizing that we are working at a much lower cognitive level. When we ask our mind to shift between a multitude of tasks constantly it gets tired.

With our fragmented, exhausted brains, we are missing out on making big and bold moves for our organizations – such as transformations. We fantasize that we are more effective, but we actually slow things down. With scattered brains we are likely to lose out on practicing our self-awareness and self-acceptance.

After a long day, I for one prefer to hang out with Netflix, going onto autopilot. You?

For us to step into self-awareness, we need to give ourselves the space and time to pause, to connect to ourselves and to sense, 'How am I right now?' As we enhance our awareness and acceptance of how we really are, we improve our health. Not only are we releasing stress, lowering our heart rate and boosting our immune system, we also strengthen our concentration, our reaction time and our memory; our capacity simply increases [(30)].

Ready for a challenge? Pause and give yourself one minute of undivided attention and feel the difference. Did it feel like a loooong time being in your own company? Did you do it?

Consider the potential of all of us being fully present in meetings. How much time could we save? How much more would we get done?

Imagine the business potential of us never being sloppy with the present moment, showing up with all we have and who we are. Imagine the benefits for our lives, and for our organizations, if we collectively enhance the quality of our presence, for our customers and everyone we touch.

Pause, connect and reflect. How does this step – Accept who I Am – make you think and feel?

Do you have a habit of thinking, 'I should be faster, sharper, a better dad or mum'? Or are you more likely to think, 'I am a great starting point for where I want to go in my life – the best and only one I have'?

Signature Practice: Check-In

It is time to bring out your transformation journal, activating your heart and hands.

Why to Check-In?

To turn Step Two into a healthy habit in your daily life, start doing Check-Ins with yourself and other people in meetings and in other interactions that matter to you, allowing you to achieve all of the following:

- **Connect** to other people, building trust and seeing the human being in everyone.
- **Become aware** of what is going on for you and other people, listening to everyone.
- **Focus** to allow everyone to become present for the topic at hand.
- **Speed** in processing and decision making, with everyone fully focused on the topic.

The practice started at the North Sea where the Check-In practice was developed by and for helicopter pilots. They used to Check-In only with the technical instruments before they took off, yet they realized that the most important Check-In they had to make to reduce risks and avoid incidents was the human Check-In.

How to Check-In?

A Check-In is usually done at the start of a meeting. Invite each of the people present to briefly Check-In by answering two questions:

- What am I feeling?
- Is there anything that could prevent me from being fully present?

You can add a third question, dependent on the situation. For example:

- What intention do I have for our time together?
- What challenges are keeping me awake at night?
- Why does this meeting/topic matter to me?

Check-Ins create value when you follow the guiding principles:

- **Right Now.** It is a moment to share what is really going on for you. Not your whole story – the essence of your now.
- **Short.** Typically, it takes only one uninterrupted minute per person while everyone listens.
- **Role Model.** The person who initiates the Check-In goes first and role models the level of openness; each person honors the rest of the team with their honesty.
- **Popcorn Style.** Other people share whenever they feel it is their time to share.
- **No Response.** A Check-In is not a dialogue. You simply say 'Thank you' everytime a person has checked-in; there is no response from anyone.
- **Ongoing.** In heated dialogues, Check-Ins are great. Ask 'How is everyone feeling now?'
- **Check-out.** At the end of the meeting, you can also briefly Check-out, with one word each, sharing what you feel now and/or where you are after the dialogue.

Pause, connect and reflect

After using the Check-In practice for a period, cement your learnings.

- What waste have you been able to eliminate for yourself with the Check-In?
- What business value has the Check-In practice created for your team?

Check-Ins help you slow down to speed up!

My wife sends her regards

'My wife sends her regards and says thanks', Jacob said, greeting me with a beaming smile. He was a very experienced and hard-working project manager. He looked so different from two months earlier when life had taken a toll on him and he had been exhausted and worn out.

'We are now having Check-Ins at the dinner table at home, every night', he added, upon seeing my puzzled expression. He shared with me how dinners had previously been a constant fight with his kids, where he had tried to force them to eat without their mobile phones in their hands, with very little success.

After we implemented Check-Ins at work, he sadly recognized that he was able to connect at a much deeper level with his colleagues than with his family. His colleagues knew better what was going on for him than his loved ones, and he decided to change that.

As a daily habit, he introduced the Check-In at the dinner table, inviting and expecting everyone in the family to be seen and heard by taking turns answering two questions: 1) What do you feel? 2) What do you celebrate from today?

This started a habit of honest sharing, which led to more joy, trust, connection, gratitude and celebration in the family, making them feel better both as parents and as children. Jacob felt he could now breathe, relax and enjoy the moment.

He realized that he too previously had too much on his mind, not being fully present with his kids. No wonder they had preferred their phones.

From Jacob's experience we learn how presence and focus in all parts of life allow you to connect to yourself and other people, a critical foundation for accepting who you are. What elements from this experience do you identify with in yourself or other people?

Presence as a business hack

What happens when we do not accept and calibrate how things are as a company?

Often external consultants are brought into a company during times of business transformation. We might complain that they tell us what we already know.

How come? Do we pretend or defend our current state?

If we do, we are creating waste and slowing our organization down. If we greenwash and avoid seeing and accepting things as they are, we will not be the one leading the change from the front. Instead, we are stalling interventions and progress.

How far are you from leading from the front in your organization today?

Fear often prevents us from tackling our real pain points. When we lose our armor and see and say it as it is - both as human beings and as businesses - we help shape the transformation, so it fits our current reality and our unique situation. We avoid following a generic transformation template that might be money wasted, even though it makes us feel safe for a while.

For this reason, one of my inspiring leaders chose to use the Check-In consistently in our executive management team meetings. He was incredibly diligent when choosing the third question in the Check-In, allowing us to come together to calibrate our current reality together.

He used it as his weekly barometer of the leadership team, as well as the business, where he understood people's intentions, concerns and resistance, detecting things he could not sense and see in business reviews, scorecards and financial reports. It became a magnificent short-cut for him, a real business hack.

I saw him becoming increasingly aware as a human being, trusting his intuition and instinct - better and better understanding where he needed to follow up and follow through afterwards, as he practiced week after week for years. Focusing on really seeing people.

As a team when we slowed down, we were able to achieve our objectives quicker. The 10 minutes' investment increased efficiency and productivity and improved decision making in the team.

Imagine those benefits realized in more teams, including yours. I have introduced the Check-In practice for everyone in every company I have engaged in. I use it as a natural part of my professional, as well as my private life and I am therefore excited to share it with you.

Always, if you are in doubt or want to accelerate your transformation, say to yourself what you know to be true: *As I slow down, I speed up.*

Have you given yourself the needed moments to pause, connect and reflect on the questions provided in this step and the previous step? It might feel like a paradox. Yet know that the more you slow down in each of the steps, the more you will speed up your transformation.

Before we move to the next step, note down your answer to the following question in your transformation journal.

In this quiet moment, what do I know to be true about me?

Step Three: I Strive for Meaning

'What is it we are questing for? It is the fulfillment of that which is potential in each of us. Questing for it is not an ego trip; it is an adventure to bring into fulfillment your gift to the world, which is yourself.'

JOSEPH CAMPBELL [31]

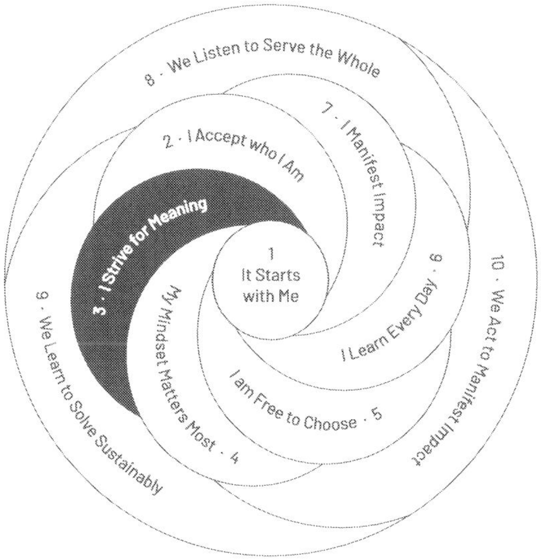

Step Three focuses on you finding meaning in your work and beyond. How do you want to bring value and contribute to other people? Creating and living guided by your meaning matters for how you experience (work) life and the impact you manifest.

Some people call this meaning, some purpose. For me it is the same. The Why of your work and potentially your life. Your meaning or purpose is personal, distinct and unique to you. Your purpose springs from the essence of who you are and that will also guide the concrete What of your work.

Knowing the deeper meaning of why you work makes you more resilient when the environment changes around you. Rather than being exhausted, as so many of us are, you give way to your voluntary and personal effort as you do what you want to do. In the midst of change, struggle and hardship your meaning lasts over time. It is a stabilizer; as the saying goes, 'A man with a strong why can bear almost any how' (32)(33).

Building a cathedral

You might say, 'I am not sure what gives me meaning and I don't have a purpose'.

Most of us are not thinking about our meaning at work every day. Understanding your meaning can be the difference between seeing yourself as a bricklayer or the person building a cathedral contributing to something grand. When I started my process of identifying my meaning, my initial thought was: 'I want to serve people's growth'.

It gave me direction, yet it was not my unique contribution and the essence of who I am. More specifically, 'I help people grow by assisting them disrupt their lives to achieve enrichment'. This means I invite people to take a walk with their fear and upsets, moving to another level of awareness, insight and consciousness.

In addition, I have chosen a unique path, distinctly fitting me, through love and laughter. I could not imagine living a day without laughter. Learning is much easier with laughter. And without love ... hmmm, unimaginable if you are me! It is the essence of who I am, irrespective of my job, what work I do and any situation I enter.

My purpose is: 'I welcome everyone to disrupt and enrich their lives - both human beings and businesses - through love and laughter'. It serves me every day, providing me with direction and inspiration. And I serve it – by doing and being who I am.

As human beings we strive for meaning, sometimes reflecting on life's big questions such as: 'Why do I exist?' and often in smaller ways: 'Why do we choose this approach for our customers?'

Do you give yourself the time to reflect upon these questions requiring a level of awareness that is a unique and privileged capacity for us as human beings?

Meaning matters

'I really don't fully see the importance of meaning', you might reflect.

When your individual purpose fits the purpose and direction of your company, you are in an ideal situation. When the opposite is true, the natural and right thing to do is part ways. You can use your purpose to guide your growth and contribution, granting you to go the extra mile in a more effortless way.

When you find and take your place, living your purpose while contributing to other people and your organization by supporting what it needs, your sense of belonging strengthens. You are in a fair exchange with your company.

Being purposeful allows us to integrate the short- and long-term with our plans – paying equal attention to the Why, How and What. Our purpose (Why) guides us to integrate the soft (How) and the hard stuff (What). With the lens of our purpose, we are able to integrate what we previously may have seen as separate, mutually exclusive, radically different or contradicting.

When engineers in a medical device division connected with their customers, understanding how the smallest design changes of the diabetes pen could make the biggest quality enhancement of life to people with diabetes, they positively changed their perspective on the tedious details of the product development process. The Why of the work, the meaning, fuels our inspiration, capacity and additional effort[33].

Can we afford it?

'Why did you only get a B in math?' my dad asked me. We were sitting in our living room. My father intensely looked at my gradebook, comparing my math grades to the rest of my grades and the grades of my brother. I shrank, and had no good answer, except that math was not my subject.

My teachers had told my parents, 'She is not her brother, Kim'. Reflecting that the teachers rated him highly because he was calm, considered and competent, and they saw me more as rebellious raw material, hurt me and I felt unfairly treated.

No, I was not Kim. I was me. My brother and I were so different - and I had no intention of becoming my brother. Instead, I was eager and absolutely determined to show that I could make it my way.

My dad taught me relativity and competition by comparing me with my elder brother and I decided to take the challenge on. He had high ambitions for all three children, including me, his middle child and only daughter. The story we were told and believed was that we were living his dream because he had never utilized his gifts fully, being smart and creative. Due to his stage fright he had never made it to any exam and therefore had never 'become somebody' in his words.

My father was my first contact with unlocked and un-leveraged potential anchored in his stage fear, which had never been tackled. What a waste of potential and human capacity it was, and I felt his struggle, wanting more and yet not daring. I grew strong with a real sense of drive as a result.

My mom and dad were having a tough time as farmers, making a living and feeding their children. They never complained; giving their kids the best possible start was highly meaningful for them.

Hardship and double working were the common denominator for them at the time I was born. Sentences such as 'Can we afford that?' 'Duty before pleasure!' 'You are what you do!' 'If you have the ability you have the duty!' became the norm and they were considered good principles and beliefs in our family. This formed a big part of my personality.

Born with an exceptional energy, I became the hardest working person you can imagine, yet often doubted myself, keeping score all the time – securing that I was 'giving' more than I was 'receiving'. I wanted to feel safe with the right to belong because 'you are what you do'. I became a workaholic, as were my parents.

I felt a strong sense of accomplishment when my head hit the pillow and I knew for sure there was nothing, not one inch more, I could have done that day. It felt safe to have taken my work to the absolute limit, yet I realize now that many of my actions where anchored in a mindset of fear and a feeling of scarcity and protection.

My insecure overachiever trait was one part of my DNA but there was an almost conflicting side of me also routed in my upbringing, hanging out with another role model and mentor who equally formed my identity.

At the age of 13, my granddad invited me to step into leadership when he, with great generosity, gave me the keys to his small business. He was renting out horses, predominately to German tourists, and my role was to optimize the business through the bookings of the horses, subsequently being the horse-back riding coach and guide.

'You can do it', he said demonstrating his blind trust in me. 'Treat our horses well and also the tourists', was his one guidance to me.

Growing up in a relatively poor household, my mom and dad had no means to financially support me, and here I was 13 years old, earning

100 Danish kroner per day in 1978! I could save and become financially independent. I felt so privileged.

I loved horse-back riding, not only for one hour but for six to eight hours a day. I loved teaching and, through that, connecting to people while becoming fluent in German. I loved being in nature. What a perfect match! 'Am I really being paid for this?' I wondered. 'I would do this for free!'

My granddad equally gave me early experiences that shaped my identity, being someone who loved my work. This part of my identity come from a mindset of love and was filled with a feeling of abundance and possibilities.

Early in life, I adopted a recipe for work: 'Be paid for what you love doing, make sure people - and horses - benefit from it and life will be good!' I quite easily mobilized my meaning with what I did and therefore work did not feel dutiful, but joyous.

These two parts of me grew up side by side, forming me as a hardworking, easy to excite, inspiring, no stop, no limits kind of leader, setting the bar challengingly high for myself and other people around me - always striving for more. Both easy to follow and hard to follow.

I have, for most of my life, worked a huge number of hours and most of the time had enormous fun too. 'Stop' and 'No' have not been part of my vocabulary and, therefore, I have benefitted from working with extraordinary colleagues and leaders with good complementary skills, such as prioritization.

In a quarterly performance dialogue, one boss, Christopher, asked me: 'How are you?' At many times in my life, I would have answered with, 'I am fine', either not being willing to check in with myself or not believing that anyone would be interested in my honest answer.

This time was different. Christopher was sitting calmly, fully present and waiting for my answer. 'I am exhausted trying to keep the overview with an endless amount of work'. I explained to him that I felt I was running two jobs.

Firstly, I was leading the Human Resources department of 500 people and secondly, co-leading the overall business transformation with more focus towards the 30.000 people in the company – inspiring and engaging our people and their leaders to embrace the change we were undergoing. Even though I enjoyed hard work, the double working was taking a toll on me.

'What do you enjoy the most?' Christopher asked, probing deeply. 'Being with the 30.000', I replied. I liked both roles and, yet, I had to admit that I loved being together with the 30.000 people the most: designing and driving the transformation from the front and connecting, listening, laughing, exchanging, enriching and being enriched. Helping 30.000 people building their Transformational Capacity connected me to what was meaningful for me in my life and the essence of me.

'Exactly!' Christopher smiled and continued, 'Why don't you recruit a deputy who focuses on the Human Resources functional role so you can put your attention on the business transformation where you impact the company significantly more and where we really need you?'

Wise as Christopher was, he highlighted my value-adding contribution, comforting my insecurity and showing me that what was meaningful for me matched what was meaningful for our company.

'But can we afford that?' I tested, carrying my family's belief, with guilt immediately creeping in.

His answer contained the absolute truth. 'I don't think we can afford not to!' He pointed to the fact that I did not look well – exhausted while running two jobs simultaneously.

He was right. I would probably have looked at stepping out of the job either mentally or physically, leading to value destruction for the company and me if we had not found a solution.

It was one of the most important conversations in my time in this company. I felt seen for who I was – helped by my leader and our conversation.

A new deputy leader joined three months later to lead the 500 people in the HR function with much grace and tenacity. Due to our great partnership, I got my life back and focused almost all my time on being fully present with the 30.000 people.

My brain fog disappeared gradually and I became more focused and creative, solving the next level of problems together with the organization. With a targeted focus from the deputy and myself, together we were able to contribute with much higher quality. We were both doing what we were passionate about and understood how that contributed to other people.

During the conversation, Christopher specifically chose to focus on how I was enjoying my work. He knew that when I enjoyed more, I would grow and contribute more, which is true for all of us.

As I tapped into my enjoyment, I found a strong link into what I found meaningful and where I could bring most value. We jointly dealt with my concern about being a failure as I was not able to do both jobs.

Throughout the conversation we dwelled on the elements needed to move from 'doing more' to 'doing less', moving from a sense of duty to joy, taking it all as dimensions of learning, not failing.

Through the process I had to let go of my old and limiting beliefs: 'I am a failure if I leave half of my job to another person' and my very favorite, 'No is not an answer '. Instead, slowly but surely, I had to embrace the value I created through the focus I gained. The hours spent at work for me after the conversation were probably the same – but felt much more effortless as I did what I wanted to do.

From my experiences with my dad, my granddad and my boss, I, firstly, learned how important it is to have great role models and leaders in your life. Secondly, I learned that when I enjoy, I create a stronger impact. Life is brief, way too brief not to enjoy.

What elements from my experience do you identify with in yourself or other people?

Matching passion with purpose

You might say, 'But we are paid, so how can we expect to enjoy as well?'

Because it is part of the formula for high performance. When every day feels like a bonus, regardless of what you are getting paid, you have found an important part - your passion, but only when you match it with your purpose.

Doing what you love doing takes you far, but peak performance is obtained only when you combine your passion with your purpose, making a valuable contribution to other people and to your company.

Passion is: 'Do what you love'. Passion asks: 'What can the world give me?'

Purpose is: 'Do what contributes'. Purpose asks: 'What can I give to the world?' [34].

We balance giving and receiving when we match our purpose with our passion. Additionally, your own passion and purpose need to match with the purpose and direction of your organization for you to be in a perfect spot. You take your rightful place and, as you do, you are less likely to feel victimized and to waste energy.

You might say: 'But not everyone can have exciting jobs!'

The meaning of a job is created by the person having it. Take Genevieve, for example. Genevieve loved interacting with people and saw it as her finest role to help and care deeply for hotel guests in her role as a concierge. She found magic in this role that many other people find trivial, bringing so much intensity and enthusiasm to her work. She always found solutions for her clients. If customers wanted something, she found it. Not simply *could* get it - but *would get it.*

Customers adored her and her warm presence and her generous effort, made from Genevieve's free will. She made the impossible possible and earned a spot in the honorable Les Clefs d'Or Club - The Golden Keys - for her extraordinary service. She was considered by far the highest performer by her hotel manager. She had matched her purpose and passion and demonstrated how peak performance can be achieved[34].

Unfortunately, not many of us are like Genevieve. Nowadays, only 15 percent of the global workforce are truly engaged. Many of us are, instead, disengaged. What a huge waste for each of us and the world[4].

Have you noticed that when you experience positive emotions, including joy, excitement, pride, inspiration and hope, it gives you energy?

That energy makes you pay more attention in meetings, engage more with customers and colleagues and contribute with new ideas, making things better. People who love what they do and know how they contribute to other people are typically the 20 percent highest performers in a company.

You might object. 'I don't want to work 60 hours per week to be among the highest performing.'

Many of us have the belief that your career is created outside 9am and 5pm and that the number of hours defines the output you create. Actually, no. It is how much you love what you do and your contribution to other people that grants you the largest capacity to perform and outperform[34].

Contrary to what we might think, joy and laughter are really good for business [35]. Thus, the question concerns how we change our mindset from duty to joy.

A question embracing the movement from a mindset of limitations – grounded in fear – to a mindset of abundance – grounded in love – for organizations and for individuals. Maslow calls this the move towards self-actualization. Other people call it: human creativity, passion, making a difference and service. They all describe the optimal state of performance where your output per hour invested increases significantly, sometimes with a factor of three or four.

Imagine the impact on business if we all expanded our output by 300 percent. This level of performance is described as being in flow, in the zone or effortless ease, all pointing at the same experience: absolute focus, absolute joy and absolute timelessness [34].

Human beings are longing and striving for where we can bring and leverage our whole self. If we do not find the opportunity at work, we will look for it elsewhere. This is a vast loss for businesses and human beings since work is such a large part of our lives and such a potent place to experience optimal performance.

Peaking through laughter

You might continue to protest: 'I get paid, so I have to be serious.'

Just know that it is a win-win for you and your company if you instead say and mean, 'I am in so much joy – am I really getting paid for this?'

I have seen people reaching peak performance when they step into enjoyment, focusing on what gives meaning, working with effortless ease, holding it light with laughter. Too little research exists regarding the impact of laughter in the workplace.

We know that laughter is great for general well-being and for health, but how does laughter impact performance?

Research suggests that humor has a positive impact with respect to performance, engagement, team cohesion, health and coping effectiveness, which leads to less burnout and work withdrawal [36].

My experience is that we hugely underestimate the impact of laughter. Some of us were brought up with, 'We are paid, so we have to be serious and are, therefore, not supposed to laugh.' Why?

Laughter makes us bond more, collaborate to a higher degree, enjoy, lighten our burdens, reduce stress, inspire hope and connect us with other people. On top of that, it is free and easy to use. I vote for laughter as a source for tapping into more enjoyment and meaning [37].

Pause, connect and reflect. How does this step – I Strive for Meaning – make you think and feel?

Are you being paid for having fun these days? Or do you become more exhausted than excited from your work? How do you see your work? 'It is my duty and I need to make a living' or 'My work is meaningful and joyful'.

Signature Practice: Enjoy

It is time to bring out your transformation journal, activating your heart and hands.

Why Enjoy?

Combining what you love doing – your passion – with how you contribute to other people – your purpose – allows you to achieve all of the following:

- **Extraordinary effort.** As you tap into what you want to do rather than have to do, you expand your voluntary effort, yet feel more excited than exhausted.
- **Outperforming.** You create a great platform to outperform yourself. Effortlessly, you go beyond expectations. Working smarter not harder.
- **Well-being.** As you enjoy, you tap into emotional wellbeing, joy and fulfilment.

Finding meaning in life is not always straightforward, but identifying what you really enjoy doing will get you there a little faster.

How to Enjoy?

Systematically removing obstacles for enjoyment enhances your value creation, tapping into not what you have to do, but what you want to do.

Reflect daily on the following questions:

- **Passion.** What did I love doing today?
- **Purpose.** How did I contribute to other people today?

Reflect quarterly on the following questions:

- **Passion.** How much is what I love doing part of my role?
- **Purpose.** What makes me and my contribution distinct and unique?
- **Enjoyment.** How do I enjoy?

'How do I enjoy?' is an impactful question; when you enjoy more, you accelerate your growth and contribution.

Have an open and honest conversation with your leader. You will be surprised as to how much influence you have on your work and role, meaning you have a real chance to shape your work for more personal enjoyment enhancing your growth and contribution.

Pause, connect and reflect

After using the Enjoy practice for a period, cement your learnings.

- How does the question, 'How do I enjoy?' disrupt and enrich your life?
- How does your company benefit from you enjoying more?
- How does enjoyment impact the growth and contribution of your company?

Enjoy being happy, healthy and high performing at the same time. It is no contradiction.

I am about to leave

Laila – a leader for four years – was convinced she was a great leader. She always felt she had successful meetings with her team where they made many decisions, really progressing well. She felt the team trusted her and each other.

We worked together for a multinational technology company and as we launched our new and enhanced performance management process, she was especially eager to try out the new third question, 'How do you enjoy?' along with the two questions she was familiar with: 1)'How do you grow?' 2)'How do you contribute?'

The first time she asked one in her team the question, 'How do you enjoy?' she was stunned by the answer.

Her team member was at first hesitant and cautious, doubting whether he should answer. Finally, he did:

'The work we are doing is really meaningful for me and I see how I can make a difference. However, there are two people in the team making my working life difficult.'

He went on tentatively to explain how two people were bullying him, although he was doing his best to avoid them. He had tried to arrive late or early to work, picking a table far from these two, but they kept teasing and chasing him, making false accusations, sharing rumors about him with the rest of the team.

He shared with Laila that even though he felt his work was so meaningful, he was looking for another job where he could make the same difference, but in an environment allowing him to feel safe. He was a great and unique contributor to the team.

Laila was devastated, partly due to the fact that she had not noticed what was going on. 'How could this happen?' she asked herself. Laila investigated the case, only to have it confirmed by the rest of the team.

Laila was curious to understand why no one had come forward earlier. The team shared that they were afraid of becoming the next bullying target if they spoke up.

This was tough feedback for Laila to receive. The team was doubting whether she would do something about the situation. She realized that she had never shared how important is was for her to create safety for the team and herself.

Laila took action. One of the two bullying team members apologetically admitted having done wrong and immediately changed his behavior. The other person refused to admit he had done anything wrong and, therefore, saw no reason to change. After further conversation without progress, Laila had to let him go.

I had the joy of watching Laila grow from this experience. She learned that not everything automatically comes to the surface and that asking questions is a dazzling way to gain new knowledge and fully understand - when you pay attention to the answers.

She realized that even if meaning is a great igniter for any person, every person has the possibility to find another place for its realization, finding an enriching environment.

What elements from this experience do you identify with in yourself or other people?

Contributing to the bigger Why of transformation

When the Why has that importance for us as human beings, what does it mean for a business?

Often business transformations slide or slow down because the bigger Why of the transformation has not been clearly defined and communicated, making it difficult for people - as an organization - to unite, operating as one force, around the transformation.

When we are not fully dialed up for the transformation, we risk being exhausted rather than excited by the hard work of transformations – as so many of our fellow workers find themselves globally today.

Not only are we missing out on engagement, we are missing out on the massive reservoir of voluntary, personal, extraordinary effort waiting to be released in every one of us – simply because we cannot stop contributing.

Instead, we waste effort on being scared when we face setbacks in a transformation. We work harder and harder, not getting to where we want to go. We de-risk the transformation when we see and take our place in driving how we uniquely contribute to the bigger Why of the transformation.

Always, if you are in doubt or want to accelerate your transformation, say to yourself what you know to be true: *What I give, I receive.*

Before we move to the next step, note down your answer to the following question in your transformation journal.

As I contribute wherever I go, how do I want to enjoy?

Step Four: My Mindset Matters Most

'The question is not what you look at, but what you see.'

HENRY DAVID THOREAU [38]

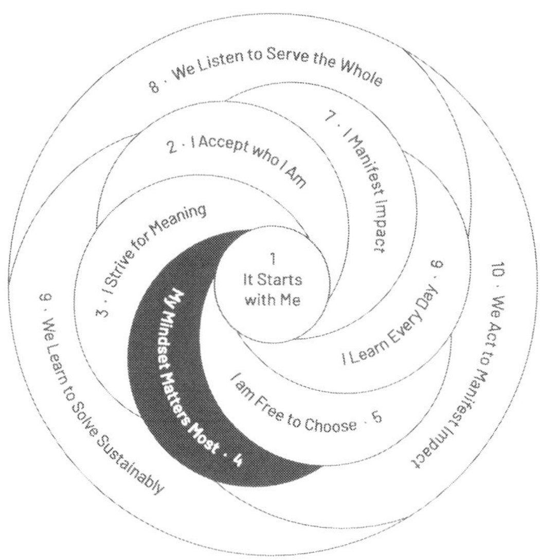

Your mind is able to move mountains and is undoubtedly the one dimension having the biggest impact on how you live your life. It is your powerhouse, your control tower. Your mind's habits are your life's habits. It runs your life.

Would you believe me if I told you that you can think yourself healthier? Would you trust me if I told you that you can become stronger by simply believing you are strong? This is true for all of us [39].

How do you typically look at the world? Is your glass half empty; do you see challenges? Tapping into the field of fear. Or is your glass half full; do you spot opportunities? Tapping into the land of love.

Your mind, by default, leans towards one of them, contributing significantly to how you experience life, including how much waste or value you create for yourself, your work and your organization.

Although as human beings we tend to have a preference – a default – we continuously alternate between these two perspectives depending on our context and what else is going on for us at the time.

We bounce quickly between these states: 'Oh no! It is raining. Everything will get wet, including me' and 'Oh, it is raining. The farmers are happy. I will bring my raincoat'.

Maybe you already sense the difference in approach regarding the output at work and in life, when you hold a mindset of fear in comparison to a mindset of love?

The surprising, and sometimes provocative, news is that your context and situation impact you much less than your general world view – your mind's habit [(40)].

If your world view is pessimistic, looking through your fear-based lens, you see one thing, whereas if your world view is optimistic, looking through your love-based lenses, you see something quite different.

In this step you are invited to become aware of your world view.

Walking with a friend in the woods

I was living in the most magnificent place in Europe, known to the local people as Paradise on Earth. On this particular Sunday, the woods of Switzerland were dressed up in their most precious autumn colors and the sun was shining. My very good friend Emma and I were walking fast, firm and far.

'Did they force you to take the job?' Emma stopped walking and looked curiously at me. 'Force me? No, of course not. I wanted the job!' I replied.

From that moment nothing was ever the same again. Right before this particular snippet of our conversation, I had spent 30 minutes sharing how hard I had been working lately, how little I had slept, how many people I was short of, how much there was to be done and what a mess the department was in.

I had listed all the problems in the new job I had taken on. Emma's question was valid. If there was so much pressure, why would her - otherwise quite sane - friend accept such a position? Her gentle and caring question brutally confronted me with my own victimhood, my Prisoner, my martyr; different names, same thing.

My new role was a promotion to Head of Human Resources and Transformation for 40 countries in a global software company. It was a big job and I felt small. I was not sure whether I would be able to live up to the role, delivering above expectations.

Having secured the job, I was now afraid of losing it. Or rather losing face, if they found out I was not qualified and therefore didn't belong to the wonderful high-performing team I felt so honored to be a part of.

At this point, I was wearing my literal and metaphorical blazer and my strategy for feeling safer was simple: I had to work harder! I had to be smarter, pretending to be on top of the world! I was not yet aware that my armor prevented me from being in true connection with other people and myself.

I did not realize that my underlying fear, my Prisoner, had taken over, telling me all the problems I had in my new job and that everything was dependent on me - the whole 30-minute story I had shared with

Emma. All the energy I had wasted in those 30 minutes had only taken me further down into my dark emotions.

When Emma, curious, probed 'Did they force you?' it became clear to me that I definitely was not forced, and I finally saw my Prisoner.

Truthfully, I had known 'she' existed for many years. She had been my loyal travel companion; despite never being fully introduced to her, I actually knew her very well. I knew what she said, how she operated, how she judged, how she complained, how she blamed and how she sometimes attacked.

'I love my job; it's great. I am so excited – and quite overwhelmed – and I am not sure if I will make it', I finally confessed to Emma.

Emma listened as I thought aloud about how I could either embrace my excitement, gratitude and awe for my new job or how I could be taken over by my anxiety and worry.

Within a single minute, I could alternate between the two world views – seeing things very differently. We both felt how the different perspectives impacted my energy. I could access positive and courageous energy, feeling the progressive intentions I had for this work, yet when I stepped into my Prisoner mode, I was pouring out negative and unproductive energy without getting anywhere. What a waste!

Emma and I broke into laughter, a huge relief. How entertaining and dramatic my Prisoner was! With her, I left the present and what was actually going on and started to fear the future. 'I wonder if they will fire me. Will I be good enough? Will they find out?'

By stepping into a mindset of love, however, I was able to focus on the present and what was actually happening – namely, that I was part of this wonderful team with this incredible boss who had given me this amazing opportunity.

I reminded myself about the wisdom from the founder of Gestalt Therapy, Fritz Perls, who taught us that anxiety lies in the gap between the present and the future[41].

From this experience I learned to recognize the voice, the energy, the world view of my Prisoner. I became aware of and understood how 'she' impacts and sometimes runs my life and of the waste I allow her to create in my life. I have also learned the healing power of meeting my Prisoner with laughter instead of blame and shame.

What elements of my experience do you identify with in yourself or other people?

The Prisoner, Tourist and Player

Do you also allow this energy waste to be part of your life?

Most of us drain or gain energy during a day when we operate from one of our three archetypes: Prisoner, Tourist and Player. Understanding, becoming aware and identifying which archetype we step into helps us to recognize fear and its waste, as well as love and its value in ourselves, in other people and in the workplace.

The Prisoner defers fault and blame to other people, always looking for an external reason for why things are the way they are. They can be outspoken and aggressive, focusing on what is wrong, and are typically not resourceful. They often use the voice of judgement.

When we take on the role of the Prisoner, it is like playing Monopoly and voluntarily sending ourselves to jail without passing 'Go' and then complaining about it. Unlike incarcerated people, we are sitting behind bars with the door open and the key in our hands.

When we activate our Prisoner, we are typically frustrating ourselves and other people. We use energy without getting anywhere. The fun is gone! Only other Prisoners want to be with us. It reduces our chances of winning significantly.

The voice of our Prisoner typically says: 'If only we had better products, I could sell much more'. 'If only management would be clearer on what they want, I would not waste my time'. 'Our IT system is lousy; I cannot use it'. 'Even if I wanted to grow, they give me absolutely no time to spend on building my Transformational Capacity'.

All this negative energy and these voices from the Prisoner serve as an objection, defense or excuse for not taking ownership for the change you want to see. In essence 'If only all other aspects but me were different than they are, I could progress'. Objections will not bring us far. What are the collective Prisoner views, energy and voices in your organization? What waste do these voices create? Do you also recognize the Prisoner in yourself?

The Tourist dabbles; they are the non-committal persons who do not take ownership. They retain the option of walking away should there be a more exciting destination, which there never is. They may learn a few phrases in the local language to be able to get by, but rarely invest in becoming fluent, as in their business life.

When we operate as a Tourist our investment into learning is never wholeheartedly and fully committed. Acting as a Tourist, our energy is low and we make life difficult for other people, not contributing with our full capacity and the required substance.

A Tourist often travel with the voice of cynicism and skeptical comments: 'Here we go again. They have defined a new program.' 'I will wait and see; they change their minds so often. Soon there will be another program.' 'Who cares? Why bother? Why me?' 'I will leave this to others as they are better at it.' 'This Transformational Capacity Program is too soft – I don't see the value. After all, I am a salesperson.'

What are the collective Tourist behaviors - also defining the culture - in your company? Do you notice them and the waste of energy and loss of capacity? Do you also recognize the Tourist in yourself?

The Player is in the game, in every positive sense of the word. The Player is committed, engaged, resourceful and resilient - focused on solving problems and taking full ownership. They thrive in collaboration, having the courage to do the right things. They are honest, sincere about how and who they are.

The Player's energy is courageous, confident, positive, optimistic. It looks forward also during hardship and other people enjoy being with them. They speak up when a change needs to happen and can be critical without pointing fingers, rather focusing at the opportunities at hand.

When we step into being a Player, we enjoy learning and building new capabilities and remaining relevant. We become the change we want to see and therefore we have many followers. As Players we act with the voice of willpower.

What are the collective Player behaviors - also defining the culture - in your organization? What is the value of this energy, voice and worldview? Do you also recognize the Player in yourself?

We all step into these three archetypes or modes in our working and private lives. You can be a Tourist one day and a Player the next, or a Player in the morning and a Prisoner in the last meeting of the day. The key to change where needed is to become aware of each of the modes as they show up, recognizing them in yourself.

The truth is that you generate limiting value as a Prisoner and a Tourist, you waste your own and other people's energy, focus and time. When you step into Player mode, you bring a courageous energy, focused on creating value and hence other Players want to hang out with you.

You might now be scanning colleagues and friends identifying who is acting as a Prisoner. It's great if you start noticing. If you are mentally pointing fingers at them, you enter your voice of judgment, entering your own Prisoner. Unless you do something about your observation by engaging with the person to support them, you are in fact operating as a Tourist.

You might reflect, 'I am not sure she will listen.'

Yes, it often takes courage! Real Players support other people becoming Players without judging them, making them aware about their behaviors for the benefit of everyone! This is a very different approach to how many organizations operate, where it is tolerated that people talk about each other instead of with each other. This means you and I tolerate it.

Do you want to continue to tolerate that? It is a destructive habit for an organization in terms of creating waste through unproductive energy and time, loss of trust and thereby speed.

As a Player you create value by holding up the mirror for your colleagues and yourself in a supportive way, thereby releasing courageous and productive energy to be used for doing great business in your team and organizations.

Feeling safe, belonging and worthy

You might say: 'But I can't control my Prisoner and Tourist. They show up unexpectedly.'

Yes, often when we expect them the least. Under the surface of the Prisoner and Tourist's pattern is fear, whereas when in Player mode, love is in our hearts and minds. When we hold a mindset of fear, it is often because we perceive that our needs have not been met or we are afraid of them not being met.

Human needs are universal and without them our ancestors would not have survived. Equally today, we want our needs to be met within a reasonable amount of time since we are better versions of ourselves when they are met.

The first and most foundational level of human need is our need for physical survival and safety, including health, nutrition, financial stability and self-defense. When we don't perceive these needs being fulfilled, we launch into fear that can lead to behaviors not directed towards meaningful outcomes, such as violence, greed, corruption, control or variations of these behaviors.

It is our perceived need that matters, not what is reality. You can be well off – even rich – and perceive that you don't have enough money. You might be greedily collecting more even if you will never be able to spend it all. Beneath the surface you are not feeling safe and, therefore, you don't have a sense of when enough is enough. You want to stay in control.

Ever met such a person? Or maybe you even recognize this is yourself? When we perceive our physical needs to be met, we can move on.

Our second level of need relates to having harmonious relationships and belonging, including family, friendship, open communication and rituals. When we don't perceive that we are getting these needs met, we step into fear, potentially turning on our blame, jealousy, judgement and conflict. You can be popular and yet feel alone. You might experience that other people have better or more friends.

Your fear of not belonging makes you divide people into 'them' and 'us', where 'us' are the insiders; people who belong. 'Them' are the outsiders; people who do not belong. You probably hang out with people who look and act like you. If you are the well-off person from before, your tribe is typically equally rich.

Ever met such a person? When you perceive that your need of belonging is being met, you can be much more inclusive and non-judgmental of people being different from you.

Our third level of needs is of building a sense of self-worth and self-esteem, including pride in self, self-reliance, excellence and positive self-image. When we don't perceive these needs as being fulfilled, we enter fear, potentially turning on our arrogance, status, power and rigidity.

You can be the best in your field and still feel that you are not good enough or feel that you are much better than the rest or have the need to be much better than the rest. The perceived unmet need possibly shows up as 'you playing small' or 'you playing big'.

You might have a tendency to say 'I did this' rather than shining the light on the people who have contributed. Or you might have a false humility, stating 'it was nothing' when, in fact, it was huge. You either hold back or take too much space, neither of them being the optimal way of creating value for you, your work and the organization.

When you perceive your need for self-esteem is being met, you are able to assess your own capacity realistically, sharing openly what you are capable of and where you need help. When needs of safety, belonging and self-worth are sufficiently met, we more easily enter our Player mode [10].

As soon as something happens – for instance, when we lose our job or get sick – we get shaken and even if it is not life threatening, it feels that way and we often move back into Prisoner or Tourist mode until reassurance returns. Finding ourselves or people around us acting like Prisoners or Tourists is an invitation to being curious around which needs are not currently perceived to be met.

Our needs being met enable us to shift focus from 'me-myself-I' to 'we-us-ours'. Yes, many people have made careers with a consistent 'me-myself-I' focus and gotten very far with that mindset. Yet embracing our Player, living a mindset of 'we-us-ours', will take us much further, to a very different and arguably much better place.

Your mindset matters most

You might ask 'What is it really that drives value or waste in my life?' The simple answer is: Your mindset.

Despite being fully empowered to change, we often, as human beings, choose not to - rather we stay safe, sometimes stuck in our old habits, beliefs and mindset, despite us seeing the waste it creates. Early on in life, I was pondering on why. Carol Dweck, American Professor of Psychology of Stanford University, provided great answers when she revealed how much our mindsets and underlying beliefs determine our lives[(42)].

We create our own experiences and our life - most of all through our mindset. We only have two mindsets to choose between: A growth mindset - what I call a love-based mindset - that propels us and where we are eager to learn, and a fixed mindset - what I call a fear-based mindset - where we are eager to stay safe and that prevents us from fulfilling our potential.

Some people are more prone to having a positive and optimistic outlook compared to other people. Studies demonstrate that significant events, like winning the lottery or being a victim of an accident, will initially impact happiness and level of optimism, but not for long. Happiness returns to the same base level both after extremely positive and negative events [(40)].

Maybe you recognize that tendency within yourself? When you receive a raise in salary, are you initially happier and after a while it feels normal again returning to the happiness level of before?

Equally, perhaps you are injured and no longer able to run in the morning as you used to. While it might annoy you, you find an alternative solution. Maybe you bike or swim as you move back to your baseline level of happiness.

We are conditioned by our usual habits of thinking. It is not who we are, but how we think that defines our baseline. As human beings we are powerfully adaptable when positive and negative things happen. Our mindset is far more important for how we experience life than what happens to us. Our emotional baseline remains relatively stable over time, unless we change our mindset.

Am I healthy or unhealthy?

You might challenge me. 'Does my mindset really determine how my life unfolds?'

Yes, to a large extent it does. In a study testing whether the relationship between exercise and health is moderated by our mindset, 84 female housekeepers working in seven different hotels were measured on physiological health variables affected by exercise.

Half of them attended a 15-minute session where they were informed that the work they do (cleaning hotel rooms) was good exercise and followed the recommendations for an active lifestyle. Examples of how their work could be seen as exercise were explained. For example, 'vacuum cleaning raises your pulse' and 'making the bed activates your core muscles'. They understood that their walking, bending, pushing, lifting and carrying was training, even though they did not go to the gym.

In the control group this information was not provided. Although the actual behavior for both groups in the study did not change, four weeks afterwards the informed group perceived that they were getting significantly more exercise. Compared with the control group, they showed a decrease in weight, blood pressure, waist-to-hip ratio and body mass index from only a 15-minute information investment!

These results support the hypothesis that exercise affects health also as placebo effect. The placebo effect is any effect not attributed to the actual event or happening, but rather attributed to our mindset, including our beliefs and expectations. The mind has a powerful influence on the body, and in some cases makes your body heal [(39)].

The first time I heard about the housekeeper study, I was stunned, realizing how my life could expand. Could it really be true that you become what you think? In fact, are you what you think?

During my Gestalt Therapy studies I became acquainted with findings where the placebo effect of any therapy amounted to more than 40 percent. Thus, a large impact is not the therapy itself, but simply the beliefs the client brings, including an expectation of whether the therapy will work and whether the therapist is able to help or not.

Imagine how the placebo influences our mindset and beliefs, impacting our whole lives to this extent all the time, and the implications this could have for how we run our businesses?

When discovering this, I worked in a large technology company, where the culture was almost breaking the company. In fact, behind the culture we found a collective mindset holding the company back rather than helping it forward, including silos fighting each other, customers being treated as objects rather than human beings and people 'greenwashing' their goals and reflecting lack of ownership. We experienced the company losing its power, its capacity, and its will.

Pause, connect and reflect. How does this step - Your Mindset Matters Most - make you think and feel?

Who is your favorite travel companion? Your Prisoner - calling out what is wrong, creating unproductive energy; Your Tourist - preserving your energy, enjoying the passenger seat; or Your Player - eager to make it happen together with other people spreading courageous energy?

Signature Practice: Activate Your Player

It is time to bring out your transformation journal, activating your heart and hands.

Why Activate Your Player?

What is your typical world view? Is the glass half empty? Do you approach situations as problems, which leads also to waste? Or is the glass half full, where you spot opportunities – creating value?

You have three archetypes: Prisoner, Tourist and Player. You might not notice them, although their voices and views impact and potentially govern your life.

- **Awareness.** Become aware of how the different archetypes play out in your personality, actions and life without judging – stepping back into imprisonment.
- **Energy.** Notice how the different archetypes impact your energy – where you waste it and where you build it.
- **Impact.** Pay attention to the effect and impact the different archetypes have on you, other people and your business.

Becoming aware is the first step needed to make the change you want to see in your life.

How to Activate Your Player?

Reflect and note down situations, circumstances, people or places which trigger the archetypes in you:

- I typically operate as a Prisoner when ...
- I typically operate as a Tourist when ...
- I typically operate as a Player when ...

How are you typically behaving (do, think and feel) being in the different archetypes?

- When I am a Prisoner, I typically ...
- When I am a Tourist, I typically ...
- When I am a Player, I typically ...

Underneath, there are often unmet needs that are triggering the archetype.

Level One: Safety

I have an unmet need of safety, existence, health, nutrition (food, water), financial stability, self-defense or ... ?

Level Two: Belonging

I have an unmet need of love, family, friendship, open communication, acceptance, sense of connection or ... ?

Level Three: Self-Worth

I have an unmet need of pride in self, recognition, respect, self-reliance, strengths, positive self-image or ... ?

Sometimes you might activate your inner Prisoner, because you lack sleep or are hungry. You might suppress needs, thinking they or you are not important, whereas when you fulfill these needs you avoid activating your Prisoner or Tourist.

In an airplane in case of an emergency you are asked to put on your own oxygen mask before helping other people. It is the same here. Taking care of your own needs will make you resourceful towards yourself and other people.

What impact does your behavior have on your surroundings when you operate from your different archetypes?

- My behavior when I am a Prisoner makes other people ...
- My behavior when I am a Tourist makes other people ...
- My behavior when I am a Player makes other people ...

How is it for you to be with other Tourists, Prisoners and Players?

- When I am together with Prisoners, I ...
- When I am together with Tourists, I ...
- When I am together with Players, I ...

You will Activate Your Player when you follow the guiding principles:

- **Awareness.** Finish this exercise often until you know yourself and your patterns of creating energy waste and value.
- **Inner detective**. Activate your inner detective to explore your Prisoner, Tourist and Player behavior and learn to recognize the difference in your energy, expression and output and your impact on yourself, your family, your work and company.
- **No blame.** Your role is to observe and increase awareness, not to blame. If you start blaming yourself, it will be harder for you to change (Step Two).
- **Share.** When you know your archetypes well, start sharing them with other people, perhaps your transformation buddy. Share how the archetypes show up for you.
- **Have fun.** Your inner Prisoner and Tourist can be highly entertaining with all their drama and waste creation - also by doing nothing.
- **Mirror.** Offer to hold a compassionate, non-judging mirror up for other people investigating their archetypes. The gift of a curious friend or colleague is priceless. In this way, you also train your Player to help other people to become Players without judgement, blame and shame.

Pause, connect and reflect

After using the Activate Your Player practice for a period, cement your learnings.

- What waste do you create when you are in Prisoner or Tourist mode for yourself, your team and your organization?
- What is the business potential of you and your colleagues showing up as Players more of the time?

The best one to hang out with is your Player.

A Prisoner hanging out with Prisoners

'I have only said "I love you" to my wife once, on my wedding day', Ethan who had been an union representative for 20 years, said to me. He looked puzzled when I shared why we wanted to bring love to the business and what I believed love had to do with it.

'I understand your hesitation ', I said. 'No one is expecting you to say "I love you" to anyone in the company; that is not the intention of bringing the heart to work. Showing up with a mindset of love in business means: collaboration instead of fighting, speaking your truth instead of avoiding conflicts, talking with and not about people and deeply caring for our customers, treating them as human beings.' I saw him relaxing now and looking curiously at me. I was impressed with his instant shift.

It took three months for his life to change noticeably after 'the heart' entered our company. 'Do you have a moment?' he asked one day at one of our leadership conferences. We sat down on a sofa in the hallway while he quietly shared. 'As an union member I often meet people who want to share negative stories about the company. I realized that I have been hanging out with Prisoners in the company, sympathizing with their viewpoints without taking a personal stand.'

He realized that, joined in collective habits of complains, judgment and negativism, Prisoners seek Prisoners. Only Prisoners want to hang out with Prisoners, often creating a subculture of spreading negative energy in the company.

He continued, 'Since I have started working with my mindset, I have found more things to be positive in the company. However, that makes me feel alone and somehow outside. Who am I going to have coffee with? I am not sure my usual tribe is interested in hearing my positive stories. What if I am actually positive? Will I still belong?'

He shared with me that the feeling of not belonging was new to him and felt at times scary. I met his growing awareness of his previous and current way of operating. He did not judge himself; he did not judge others. His calm and productive energy was permeating our conversation.

During the next four to six months I witnessed him finding his foothold, his voice. Slowly but surely at his own pace and in his own style, he tiptoed into this new world. A journey I had the deepest respect for. Then he decided to walk alone, moving away from his usual tribe only to realize after a while that many people chose to follow him on the new path. Yet when he started his journey, he had no guarantees.

From Ethan's experience we learn that our mindset is impacted by our context and surroundings, sometimes making change harder. Equally, with our mindset and behaviors, we also impact our context and surroundings. What in this experience do you recognize in yourself or other people?

Resentment can pull a company down

Can our collective mindsets make or break a company? Yes, absolutely. As the American author and consultant Peter Drucker famously expressed: 'Culture eats strategy for breakfast.'

Mindset has the power to destroy and equally build a company; consequently, in the technology company we offered education to everyone around mindset and how mindset matters most! Firstly, the engineers reacted with apprehension, although talking about our three archetypes (Prisoner, Tourist and Player) was something everyone was able to connect with and relate to.

It made a significant difference to our company when we became aware of the mindset we held as individuals and collectively. The vast majority of us were able to identify our Prisoner, Tourist and Player, including reflecting on the impact they had and how we showed up. From this foundation of awareness, we worked on shifting our mindset into a Player mode to create a new culture for the company.

Realizing the positive effect this had on my life and on the companies I have worked for, I wish and expect you to be positively affected by your exploration of your mindsets.

Many business transformations fade or fail because the organization - meaning you and I - resents, resists and rejects it. Resentment, resistance and rejection is the unproductive and destroying energy of a Prisoner and a Tourist - an energy that we might not even notice because we are so used to it.

Too many of us simply stay in Tourist or Prisoner mode for too long, with the risk of pulling the company down by our lack of real ownership. Human and business transformations always require all of us to unlearn old beliefs and mindsets - adopting a loving and learning mindset for us to be able to constantly evolve.

What can unfold when we meet the needs behind our Prisoner and Tourist modes? Well, the endless complaints from a Prisoner often reflect strong desires, intentions and aspirations. When the previously negative energy - always creating waste - is turned into positive and courageous energy - always creating value - it is like a fountain of capacity for the individual as well as the company.

The energy of a Tourist is often much lower - holding back, carefully observing and self-preserving. As Tourists we can stop the flow in a company. Imagine showing up as a Tourist when meeting your customers.

Will you miss listening to their needs and bringing good value to them and therefore to the company? Will you sell to them the simple solution - the one you know?

When assisting each other in putting the Tourist to rest, we release energy that otherwise would not be activated. Waking up from being a Tourist is to be rejuvenated and revitalized.

Always, if you are in doubt or want to accelerate your transformation, say to yourself what you know to be true: *I create my own reality; I change my mind, I change my life.*

Before we move to the next step, note down your answer to the following question in your transformation journal.

When I view through the lens of love, what am I seeing?

Step Five: I am Free to Choose

*'It is not the freedom from conditions,
but it is freedom to take a stand toward the conditions.'*

VICTOR E. FRANKL [43]

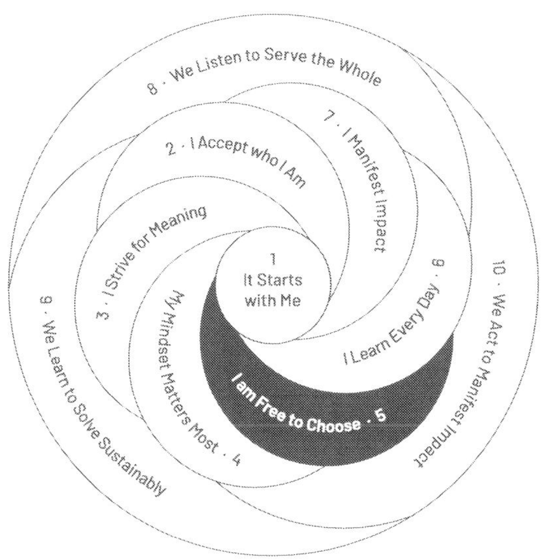

Step Five takes you into the essence of this book: becoming aware of your freedom to choose between fear and love. You learn to move from a mindset of fear to a mindset of love, or rather through fear to love, even when you are tested in the most difficult circumstances. This step equips you to turn upsets into setups for learning, to experience how disruptions can accelerate enrichments.

Even when you see no options in the most challenging life situations, choices in every moment are available and when you realize this, your life's capacity significantly expands. Will you give yourself time and freedom to choose your response?

Business transformations often appear as challenging life situations for companies where problems are complex, options seem limited, competitors are many, dilemmas are increasing, stakeholders' needs seem to diverge and everyone is increasingly nervous, impatient and even fearful.

I've heard it said that life is 10 percent what happens to you and 90 percent how you react to it. While I don't know for sure if 10 percent is accurate, I have observed in myself and many other people how, by far, the largest part of our life is determined by how we respond to what happens to us. Consider the negative energy we all use and spread when we react to life and the positive and productive energy we use and spread when we act in life. In both cases we create a ripple. Very different ones.

Do you find yourself blaming your circumstances when things are difficult?

We do not always have a choice about what happens in our life. But we always have a choice about how we respond to it. I can't remember ever talking with CEOs and senior leaders who did not know that the root of their major challenges was created by themselves and their organization. With our choices we tend to either hinder or help progress.

What would happen to you and your life if you choose to pause and become aware of two dimensions before you (re)act in heated situations?

1) How are you entangled with the surrounding world: what is yours and what belongs to the surroundings?
2) What emotions are going on for you? When you have answered those questions - then ask yourself the essencial question: What would be a loving response – to myself and other people?

Have you ever received an email that made you see red? Have you ever immediately responded with an answer that you later regretted?

In the heat of the moment you did not feel you had a choice in the very few seconds it took for you to answer, After a while, you might realize that your reactions were out of proportion with the situation.

Your transformational work is rarely about the situation – in this case the email – rather it is your reaction that is 'the work'. What is going on for you? And the more you don't want to study your reactions, the more value it will give for you to do so.

What waste did you create? Did you end up harming a relationship, saying something you did not really mean? A seemingly small incident having implications for you, your colleague and the environment in general.

Losing my work and losing it

It happened to me when writing this chapter. I had been scribbling for two full days, happy with my achievement; I felt complete. When I opened my computer discovering that I had lost my file, I literally lost it. I panicked. Two days of work was gone!

My fear kicked in that I would not be able to remember what I had written. Most of all, I feared that the time wasted would stress me out! Dark thoughts poured over me. Michael, my partner, offered me help, but I was too upset to let him in. Instead, I snapped at him, rejecting him – becoming even darker in my mind. He was disappointed with me and I was too.

I wanted the file back! I wanted to be different than I was, and I did not want to hurt Michael and yet, it was all I did. Indeed, I catapulted back to work with Step Two: I Accept who I Am.

Blaming myself for not having taken the time to make a backup. I had just been busy writing. After a while I managed to pause and calm down, especially when I connected to why I was writing and the dreams I had for my book.

The natural consequences were clear: I had to respect and care for my writing-work. I was reminded about my teacher's words: 'Love is a way of being'. A choice you make moment for moment. Are you caring and showing gratitude towards the clothes keeping you warm? Are you appreciating the table and chair that help you eat comfortably? Are you taking care of the documents that carry your stories? Hmmm. I realized that there is still some work for me to do.

I recognized my behavioral pattern from before - overreacting when my time is being challenged. It happens when people, including myself, are late, do not get to the point and are not well prepared.

Wasting time is a real trigger for me, never feeling I have enough of it. Since I was a kid, I have felt short on hours, given what I wanted to achieve in life. Wouldn't it be ideal if a day had 26 hours? Talk about not accepting things as they are (Step Two). Losing two days of work was also hard for me, used as I was to evaluating myself through the lens of 'You are what you do'.

Overtaken by fear and furious, I literally felt my brain collapsing. I couldn't stay fully focused on solving my problem. I did not see any solutions when I was busy with not wanting to have lost the file, which obviously was a distraction for the brain and a complete waste of energy and time - exactly what happens when fear takes over your brain.

More so, I was wired up for the rest of the evening, preventing me from stepping into my creative writing space writing with flow, ease and joy. My resourceful and productive energy and space was lost, leading to even more time and energy loss. I let my limiting belief steer me, a story I had kept telling myself for years and obeying it as the truth: 'I must spend my time effectively for me to be accepted'.

Had I paused and taken a deep breath, I might have been able to put a fresh perspective on my limiting belief, understanding that this story was no longer serving me. I might have had the capacity to welcome a new and reframed story encompassing an appropriate and empowering belief: 'I enjoy the time I have, seeking a natural flow in my work'.

Boy, did I meet my own humanity showing me that I am never done with the Ten Steps that evening. You and I will keep meeting each other in the steps and keep revisiting them during our lives, thankfully with more and more capacity to understand the essence of each step, as we move to a higher level of awareness.

From my experience, I learned how important it is to pause, breathe and let the pause work for me. That slow down gives me the time to become aware that I am indeed free to choose my response in each moment, even when I am triggered, even when it does not feel like that at all. Realizing that when I don't, the waste I create is significant.

Am I alone? Have you had similar experiences where you have been taken over by your feelings and thoughts?

Being hijacked by triggers

When are you most triggered?

A trigger is also termed by the father of Emotional Intelligence Daniel Goleman as an amygdala hijack. It is an emotional and physiological response that is immediate, overwhelming and out of proportion with the actual stimulus - triggering an accumulated memory of pain and pleasure referring us back in time to situations which have not been fully resolved.

We react disproportionately to the situation, carrying baggage from the past we have not dealt with. We might not even know it is there. We need to work on the baggage, not the triggers nor the situation or person that initiated the trigger [28].

An amygdala hijack forces us to pay attention, claiming: 'This is urgent, you need to react immediately' and so you do, without thinking twice. The reaction is binary: 'Do I eat it, or does it eat me?' The emotional response overrides the brain in a millisecond. A hijack includes three parts: 1) strong emotions, 2) a sudden unpleasant reaction and 3) post-episode realization that the reaction was inappropriate. Some people never reach the third part; they keep justifying their reactions and that they are right [14].

We know all too well from experiences with our families that when we are caught by an amygdala hijack, even our loved ones, in effect, turn into our enemies. We go straight into fight, flight or freeze mode and from there we lose reason, logic and love. You probably have experienced that nothing is resolved as long as you are triggered or hijacked.

The first stage in handling our triggers is to become aware of these automatic reactions. Only then we can start interrupting our patterns; for example, when I realized that I have a pattern with time and a belief that: 'Time must be spent effectively for me to be accepted'. We all have these limiting beliefs, reducing our perspective, flexibility and resilience.

When we pause and become aware of our automatic reactions, we are able to change and rewire limiting beliefs and stories that may not be serving us any longer into more empowering beliefs and stories. For example, as I realized that my story 'Time must be spent effectively for me to be accepted' was no longer helpful, I instead reframed my beliefs to 'I enjoy the time I have, seeking a natural flow in my work'.

Brain science shows that it takes six seconds to circumvent the hijack, allowing us to halt the full adrenaline, cortisone rush that overtakes us. By pressing our inner pause bottom, we can circumvent this amygdala hijack and access our more mature thinking and rational brain, allowing us to step back into reasoning, to perspectives and logic where danger and drama lose grip on us [28].

You might challenge me: 'Why should I care?'

So much good energy is being wasted due to our upsets – for example, in my case: collaboration, help, concentration, focus, creativity, productivity, relationships and wellbeing. The trigger often tells you what is important to you; if not, you would not be triggered. It is time to switch on your inner detective to discover what is behind your triggers. What is really going on? What is really important to you?

Your triggers are illustrations of the idea that only a small part of life is what happens to you, whereas the biggest part is how you choose to respond to what happens to you. Imagine my incident scaled to 10, 100, 1.000, 10.000 or 100.000 people and the potential for you and your colleagues to learn how to handle your triggers as they occur.

In a triggered state you are not able to solve the many and complex challenges you face as your brain collapses. You cannot see what you need to see, and you cannot solve what you need to solve with a reduced brain and body capacity.

Consider all the brain and body capacity you lose to drive innovation, to solve problems, to focus on customers. Relationships being harmed, collaboration and engagement being hampered. The time, energy and focus gained by not blaming and shaming is significant.

As you become aware of your human conditioning, you can choose to respond differently to things happening to you. This is a big idea! Most of us are triggered several times a day – by countless people and situations. You might notice it as frustration, anger, withdrawal, tiredness.

When you are triggered, your Prisoner and/or Tourist show up in all their glory, and as your world contracts, your Player is nowhere to be seen on the horizon.

Physical pain overtaking

You might be challenging me: 'I don't see I have choices and that my choices can change me.'

Let's look at an example. Joe injured his neck while doing heavy-duty electrical work The surgery did not go well, and he suffered chronic pain that left him unable to do the job he loved. His family was dependent on his income, which was now at risk. Joe was angry, worried and frustrated and his pain was destroying him.

Fortunately, he was brave enough to attend a program encouraging him to choose to step into gratitude and a positive attitude, working on keeping his hope alive, letting go of his anger and creating reasonable expectations.

It was hard, emotional work for Joe and his recovery was remarkable, emphasizing how a positive attitude can relieve your pain and life. Joe went back to his work, his family and his life almost fully recovered from his pain.

Research substantiates how to treat chronic pain through attitude, mindset and life perspective in combination with - or even without - painkillers. When patients adopt an attitude of gratitude, for example by repeatedly expressing gratitude for being given an opportunity for recovery, they experience less pain [(44)].

Gratitude has the power to heal, energize and transform lives. It requires courage, combined with self-compassion to change our automatic patterns. I often leverage humor and lightness, not taking myself too seriously, helping me to become creative in shifting into a more empowering belief.

Pause, connect and reflect. How does this step - I am Free to Choose - make you think and feel?

Are you often in a situation where you feel or say: 'Why me? Why does this happen to me again?' Or are you more likely to think or say: 'What is going on here? What are my options? How can I best respond?'

Signature Practice: Press Pause and Shift

It is time to bring out your transformation journal, activating your heart and hands.

Why Press Pause and Shift?

When you get triggered by a person or situation that instantly makes you annoyed, frustrated, anxious or stressed, the best you can do is to Press Pause, which allows you to reach all of the following:

- **Awareness.** Build awareness around your initial responses and feelings for you not to jump straight to withdrawing, blaming, judging or mistrusting.
- **Choice.** Once you Press Pause, you have the opportunity to make a choice as to how to respond.
- **Resourcefulness.** When you consciously choose how to respond to your triggers, you build resilience and resourcefulness.
- **Connection.** Allows you to stay connected with yourself and other people, even in challenging situations.
- **Your best.** You interrupt unhelpful responses, such as getting stressed, frustrated or anxious, choosing to be at your best by acknowledging what is important to you.

How to Press Pause and Shift?

You work through four stages when you are triggered.

1) **Press Pause**
   Being resourceful means having many different strategies for Pressing Pause.

   - **Gap.** Take a breath; count to 10
   - **Help.** Speak to a friend; ask for help
   - **New context.** Go for a walk; take a break; sleep on it
   - **New perspective.** Think positively; notice your emotions without judgement
   - **Share.** Build trust by sharing what is going on for you; for example: 'I am super triggered, and I know, I ... ' (owning it, not blaming other people)

2) **Notice your trigger**
   Although you may not be able to influence the situation or person, you recognize that it is your trigger and your emotions.

   - What is my trigger?
   - What can I really observe and what belongs to my perception?
   - What is important to me and what needs of mine might not be met?

3) **Make your shift**
   You identify what you need to 'let go of' and what you want to 'let come'.

   - What limiting beliefs and stories do I need to let go of?
   - What could be new and empowering beliefs or stories supporting my shift?

4) **Make your choice**
You consider your options, make a thoughtful and heartful choice and take ownership of how you respond and behave.

- What experience do I want to create for other people and for myself?
- What choice do I have in terms of my response to the situation?

Pause, connect and reflect

After using the Press Pause and Shift practice for a period, cement your learnings.

- What is the value for you, your team and your company when you Press Pause and Shift?

The more you Press Pause and Shift, the better you will become at it. Like any other practice, it requires practice.

This pause with a shift has the power of changing the outlook for your day and your life.

How is this a gift?

Both John and I worked for a multinational company and exactly at the time when John took over as CEO, a shit storm hit the company. The media were accusing the firm of being the 'bad guys', pointing at activities that happened 10 years ago.

John, not being with the company back then, was alone in the firing line, confronted with all the aggression, accusations and blame. It went on for weeks and weeks, with the company on the front page of various papers as 'the bad guys'.

Four weeks into the storm, one autumn afternoon he inched into my office, worn out, sharing how he felt unfairly treated, the harm it was doing to his family, how they were reacting and how he felt torn to publicly explain that he had not been the one causing the problems. 'Why me?' he groaned. He was triggered, feeling unfairly treated.

As he said it, he realized that feeling like a victim now would not help him or anyone. He was able to pause by saying it out loud. We sat together quiet for a while – indulging in the power of him 'owning it'. 'How can this experience become a gift?' I gently tested. He looked stunned. 'A gift? What do you mean?'

He thought about this and slowly he shifted his perspective, turning the upset into a setup for learning. As a CEO and a human being, he had to let go of his limiting belief that he would only have to stand up for what had happened under his watch. Instead, he had to embrace life as it is: life is neither fair nor unfair – it simply is.

Together, we captured the major benefits of the situation for him, including becoming very clear about his integrity and celebrating that he was not passing on the bug to his predecessor, which he could easily have done.

Most importantly though, this was a platform for him to realize his biggest dream of making this company an ethical company, doing well while doing good and being a role model for the rest of the industry.

When John saw how this upset could connect to his meaning and purpose, he lit up. I will never forget him stepping out of my office, giving me a thumbs up while he happily repeated: 'This is a gift, this is a gift'.

It was one of the most graceful shifts and learnings of 'surrendering to what is' that I have witnessed in a painful situation that then turned lighter.

From John we learn how even in difficult situations we have the freedom to choose how we respond, and with our choice we can turn a challenge into an opportunity - seeing an upset as a setup for learning and as a gift. What in this experience do you recognize from yourself or other people?

Transformations require many choices

How can triggers impact business transformations?

During human and business transformations, there are many opportunities to be triggered by the increased demands and competing forces a transformation encompasses. When we work with our individual and collective triggers, undergoing significant transformation, we want you and I to step into freedom, not feeling imprisoned in our own working lives and within the transformation.

One of the choices to make is whether the transformation and company is one for you. It is unlikely that you are forced to stay in one role, in one company. If you feel imprisoned, it is time to change your mindset or your context.

Many business transformations are challenged by the lack of choices at all levels in the organization. Trapped in fear we beat around the bush – asking for more data and information, stalling or delegating decisions that need to be taken. It is as if we don't understand that making no decision is also a decision.

When too many people are avoiding taking decisions, a cautious, hesitating and therefore value destroying organizational culture develops. Successful transformations require an endless amount of daily decisions.

From a loving mindset we need to take conscious choices anchored in our understanding of the root causes of our challenges. We have the freedom to choose our responses in any moment and never to accept sloppiness.

Always, if you are in doubt or want to accelerate your transformation, say to yourself what you know to be true: *My choices are mine to live!*

Before we move to the next step, note down your answer to the following question in your transformation journal.

As I pause, connect and reflect, what choices do I want to make now?

Step Six: I Learn Every Day

'There can be no learning without action, and no action without learning.'

REG REVANS (45)

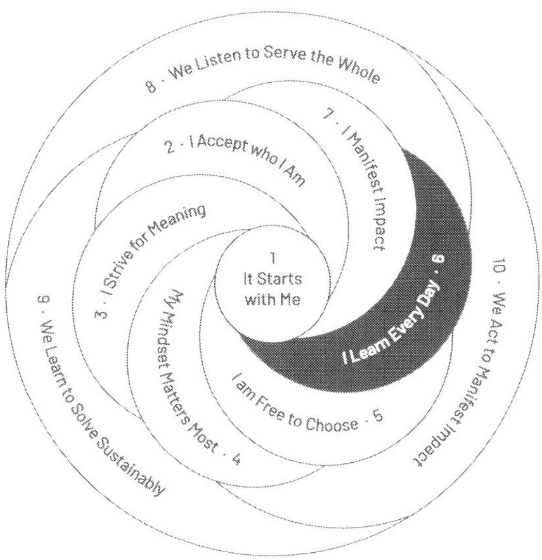

A trigger or upset can break or make your day! It depends on how you respond to the upset – as we learned from John. When adopting a mindset of 'Every day is learning' you are likely to turn upsets into set-ups for learning – as one important element of learning.

Learning every day requires you to hold a mindset of love rather than a mindset of fear, welcoming failure as one of many inspirations for learning. You learn to understand that fail does not stand for Flops, Accidents, Incidents and Low points. It means First Attempt In Learning. From a loving and learning mindset you start seeing failures as gifts.

From the field of fear, you might label something as a mistake, whereas seeing them as miss-takes is an opportunity to take a deep breath and ask: 'How do I learn from this?' and 'What can I not miss taking from this experience?'

Mistakes might trigger you, requiring you to slow down, exploring your triggers by asking: 'What does my reaction to the mistake tell me about myself?'

It is not the mistake that is interesting, but rather what you discover about yourself studying your reactions, including how you are judging, defending, camouflaging, avoiding or labeling.

What difference would it make in your life if you instead looked at mistakes with curiosity, courage and self-compassion to step into learning?

Grow by failing fast

Can you possibly see your failures as an investment in your future?

You would not be the first to walk that path. The club of successful people learning from their failures is large.

In 1993, the Harry Potter author J.K. Rowling was an unemployed single mother who saw herself as a failure. This perspective of failure allowed her to strip away the inessential and stop pretending to herself that she was anything other than what she was.

She began to direct all her energy towards the only work that mattered to her. Living on benefits in a flat in Edinburgh with the daughter she adored, she had an old typewriter and a big idea. Harry Potter has now sold more than 500 million copied worldwide, making it the best-selling book series in history, and Rowling has become a celebrity.

And she is not alone.

The groundbreaking medical drug penicillin was discovered when Alexander Fleming accidentally forgot to put his petri dish with staphylococcus in the incubator. He left it at the lab bench and went for two weeks of vacation. A penicillium mold spore had accidentally come into the medium and when the temperature was right, the mold spores grew. Today, penicillium has saved millions of lives [46].

Highly successful people are often the ones who have failed the most and those who are not afraid of admitting their failures [47].

Steve Jobs was asked to leave Apple due to his controlling leadership style. Pushed out of the company he had worked so hard to grow into a recognizable brand, he took it as a personal failure. Before returning to Apple, Steve Jobs, with his usual intensity and courage, founded NeXT and spun Pixar off into its own entity.

By the time he returned to Apple, 12 years after he had left, he was a much more mature leader. He consciously worked on tempering his obsession with control and thereby became much better at empowering talented employees to do what they do best.

His change in leadership style was a contributing factor in Apple's revival after it suffered major setbacks during his absence from the company [48][49].

You might object: 'But I really don't like failures.'

It is human but not helpful. You are prone to avoiding failures since they could have cost you your life 200,000 years ago. Eager to avoid failures you might find yourself – without bad intentions – holding onto situations that are not working, only to make them worse as time passes and the impact of the failure increases.

Being aware of this you can actively choose to work with your fear, to embrace it and shift into a learning mindset. When you learn to fail fast, you will be able to save energy, time and money. But not only that: You can turn failures into opportunities for constant evolution and adaptation.

Kleenex napkins were originally marketed to remove makeup. Only when women began complaining that their men were blowing their noses in their makeup removers did the company realize that the market was much bigger. Post-it Notes were originally marketed as bookmarks. Very useful, but soon found to be relevant for much more.

Would you see these stories as failures or future fortunes if they were yours?

With a learning mindset you are not afraid to move into action, understanding that in the action there is learning. Once you see more as learning, you strengthen your learning muscle. This requires a daily workout, like any other muscle you want to strengthen. The ability to learn allows you to sense, adjust and constantly progress in line with what you and your business transformation need.

Another way of learning

You might object: 'I don't have time to learn every day'.

And what if I told you this investment will soon save you time? Today, we have to reinvent our skill-set and competencies again and again [(22)]. The education we have will most likely be obsolete five years from now [(50)].

The Fourth Industrial Revolution represents a fundamental change in the way we live, work and relate to each another. The changed pace of our working routines and thereby what we need to learn is determined by the pace of technology advancements, often happening exponentially.

One-third of the workforce or 800 million jobs might be displaced by 2030, yet no one knows exactly how that will play out. Some jobs will be taken on by robots, Artificial Intelligence, 3D printing and other technologies; other jobs will change, and new jobs will evolve, being dramatically different in character and requiring different skills, competencies, behaviors and mindsets[51].

You might wonder: 'Will I have a job? Will I be able to grow fast enough to belong? Will I be good enough? Will I remain relevant?'

These are good questions, given the pace of change. Transformations offer challenges and growth prospects for most of us. As human beings we have proven again and again how resilient and adaptable we are.

Equally, in the Second and Third Industrial Revolutions, great job losses were predicted and happened, yet unemployment did not materialize as expected since new jobs were created. The challenges then turned into opportunities for us, companies and societies. A strong learning mindset will help you to become a part of the future workforce.

You might wonder: 'I already have my good education – what more is there to learn?'

Learning the art of transformation is very different from learning the science of engineering, finance or technology. The process of 'learning how to learn' might be your most important learning object.

Learning can be seen as horizontal and vertical. Horizontal learning happens when we learn to speak languages, when we accumulate knowledge, skills and competencies. It is learning at the same level – focusing on building knowlegde. This is what we learn in traditional schools and education [52][53].

Vertical learning, on the other hand, is not about acquiring exact knowledge but about knowing otherwise. Vertical learning makes us grow with questions. It cannot be studied – it has to be experienced.

We are used to studying math, project management or physics – but not ourselves. When we learn vertically, we study and transform how we think, feel and make sense of the world. We jump in consciousness and awareness to another level. *How* you know now becomes more important than *what* you know.

When you learn vertically you increase your capacity to recognize patterns or systems across multiple data streams. You might be sensing the emerging trend of what happens around you when you start changing yourself; you might be seeing the opportunity behind win-win solutions for the first time - or solving a complex problem you could not solve before. You learn different skills like staying stay calm while working in uncertainty and complexity. You understand that controlling and comprehending everything is impossible and asking for help essential for progress.

Whereas horizontal and vertical learning are complementary, vertical learning is becoming increasingly important in the Fourth Industrial Revolution and essential in The Heart Revolution.

With this book you have enrolled in the School of Transformation where you learn new qualities such as collective intelligence, integrity, creativity, resilience, global thinking, courage and your ability to reinvent yourself - all captured in a mindset of love and vertical learning.

No major education will teach you that. However, you only learn it as you practice the Ten Steps of Transformation, engaging with increasingly complex situations.

Your ticket to the future is your total learning agility, which allows you to build Transformational Capacity. Know that it is never the size of the gap that matters, but your ability to close the gap with speed. Learn, unlearn, relearn again and again and again.

Everything is learning and learning is everything

My mom claims that I was born hungry for learning. Learning at the pace I desired was not easy while living in the countryside far away from everything and everyone. Yet I remember brilliant moments of wonder and exploration.

My first inspiration into understanding facets and meaning of life as well as the field of transformation came through my mom's bed-time reading of the Danish author H. C. Andersen's fairy tales, revealing lessons of life, life's dark corners and big beautiful boulevards. Tales telling how hardship and upsets can have happy endings. With his simple, accessible, inclusive and yet profound stories, H. C. Andersen inspired and united me and my mom – as he has done with many families around the globe for more than 100 years. Through these quiet moments with my mother, my interest for the nature of life was piqued very early.

At the age of seven, I joined a voluntary pre-school and the first day was the closest to heaven I could imagine. My mother asked me at the end of the first day if I wanted to continue at this school. 'Can we afford it?' I replied, knowing that we did not have much money for anything but food. 'Yes, it is free', my mother confirmed. 'Unbelievable!' I thought paradise had indeed arrived.

I loved every day, every hour of my time in that school and I cried when the roads were closed because of snow, making it impossible to attend. School became my hobby from the very first day and I literally did not leave school for the next 30 years, except for one year of traveling. I studied one subject after the other. All the education as well as all the assignments ... even all the exams ... I enjoyed. These learning communities became my communities. My tribe.

Still today my magic moments are when people do something they did not think was possible or when they understand something new and novel. I am simply collecting light bulb moments.

Lifelong learning

You have followed my journey from being a coconut to becoming an avocado leader. It did not end there. In fact, transformational journeys never end.

A couple of years ago, I was co-leading a significant corporate transformation where I, for a while, had been sharing with people how important I felt it was to embrace everything as a chance to learn. Then one of my own biggest lessons hit me unexpectedly like a boomerang.

I had given an interview to a newspaper about the essence of transformation in which I was asked about my personal inspirations. I shared the names of both famous and infamous world leaders, choosing also to name an evil dictator, intending to include him only as a warning for history not to repeat itself, while stressing the huge negative impact he had.

A journalist from another media outlet picked up the story, shared it around the world, and created 320,000 clicks from it in one day. This new - second - article used my example of reverse inspiration as the headline without using the caveat I had included to explain my full reasoning for including the dictator, and I felt manipulated.

I was angry and disappointed, but I also had to take a hard look at myself: I alone had approved the wording of the original article without pausing long enough to consider it from multiple perspectives and cultures. Therefore I had not seen the risk of this being used out of context and without the caveat I felt was important.

Mentioning the dictator's name as a source of any kind of inspiration would justifiably be perceived as insensitive. I just didn't pause for long enough then to see it as the words came out of my mouth in the interview.

As the wave of anger hit me from everywhere, I really understood that any time you use a mass murderer's name, in any context, then you're bound to lose, whatever your intent. Certain names and deeds can never be neutral, which is why they also never can be allowed to appear alongside examples of kindness. I learned something blunt and inflexible about context and perspective. I saw how certain names from history only serve to kill any kind of attempt to be clever. Period.

Following publication of the second article, I experienced many different emotions, including my own anger, frustration and disbelief, but also, from others, connection, consideration, support and care.

It was hard for me to face how I had thoughtlessly hurt many people, and this made me feel guilty for a long time. I went public, sincerely apologizing for having done so, as well as making it crystal clear that I am absolutely against what this dictator had done.

Processing all that happened was a lengthy journey with plenty of ups and downs, in which I accepted total responsibility. I owned it. Without blaming others, even if my intention was nowhere to be seen in the second article, and even if I felt I had been misunderstood. It was still my own stumble.

Even today, I feel vulnerable in sharing and retelling this event as an important lesson in my life. The same questions as before reappearing: Will I be judged? Will I be misunderstood again? During moments like that, I remind myself that every setback is an opportunity to learn and indeed, I took away valuable lessons from this experience, even if it hurt.

First, never miss a moment to meet people with kindness. I received so much unexpected kindness after this happened, and it had a huge impact on me. It was a new experience to fully take it in, to welcome all the love and care I received, which only served for me to more fully appreciate 'my avocado'.

Second, never miss breathing and pausing, thinking with compassion about others before expressing thoughts. Third, always nurture the way of regarding any situation with love; I realized how easy it was for me to return to fear, and how my perspective and capacity immediately changed as I remembered.

And, lastly, I was put in mind of what a wise colleague said: 'This might be important for you, and you think it is the end of the world, but other people have moved on, being busy with what is important for them.' For me, this final message was revealing. It was a relief to realize that my sorrows were not the center of the world.

Life is our teacher and our biggest upsets have the potential of being our greatest teachers when we choose to see them as learning. Sometimes the teachings come when we least expect them; the learning can be light and sometimes terrifyingly tough. I learned an enormous amount from this experience, and I prefer the person I am now.

What upsets in your life have turned into strong platforms for learning?

A whole in the performance ceiling

You might ask: 'But does all this learning not distract me from performing?'

No actually – rather, learning facilitates peak performance. As we step up in our life, into a new job, a new ambition or vision, most of us face fear at some moment. When we are in the field of fear, our fixed mindset, our reptilian brain, takes over. This typically happens when we are too challenged or under too much pressure [(54)].

We orient ourselves around problems and threats trying to defend ourselves against what is happening – engaging with our Prisoner – or we withdraw passively letting our Tourist run the show.

Whereas our Prisoner and even our Tourist drive actions and can enhance performance for a period, they have a clear ceiling. We work to react to problems, to deliver perfect outcomes, typically focused on what is needed to achieve approval from above, focused on moving up within our organization.

Our focus is to make us feel safer, to eliminate fear, which never leads to peak performance. It is designed to maintain, has a ceiling and holds little extra energy beyond 'I have to', a mindset of 'playing not to lose' and 'there is only one winner'. We have a pie of a certain size and if you take a bite, I lose mine; the mindset of 'win-lose' and of 'scarcity'.

When in the land of love - with a growth mindset - we orient ourselves towards our purpose and passion, making us more daring and curious, receptive to learning and of the opportunities ahead. With our uniqueness as human beings follows our individual dreams and desires of how we want to contribute in our jobs, teams, businesses and in our life. How we want to make a difference and how we want to contribute and create, requiring us to risk our safety, belonging and status, to lean into learning, and to leave our comfort zone for self-actualization.

Actions driven by purpose and passion create better outcomes as they come from a different place inside us (Step Three). With passion and purpose, and our desire to learn, we blow a hole in the ceiling of our performance as we tap into a very different pool of energy and engagement, driven not by 'I need' but 'I want'. Here we are playing to contribute, happy to learn, to win without needing everyone else to lose. The pie simply expands - endlessly - and we all have a piece of it.

'Okay, I got it. How do I best set myself up for learning?' you might ask.

Creating a positive learning environment for yourself is your first task. As human beings we respond more strongly to negative events, including feedback, than positive [55].

A study demonstrated that more than half of the people who had received overly harsh criticism from a colleague or a leader decided intentionally to decrease productivity by decreasing their work effort, time and quality. Have you ever experienced that moment where your inner voice first yells 'Get lost! I am not going to do it' or 'Who do you think you are?' and then you deliberately choose to reduce your effort as it is not being valued anyway[56]?

Purely harsh feedback is unhelpful, whereas balanced feedback is beneficial. It allows you to chew and act on it. Your attitude towards learning and feedback determines how much you learn from the feedback.

When focusing on what is working instead of remediating what isn't working, you are likely to learn more. In an experiment, scientists split students into two groups. The first group was provided with positive coaching; the students were asked about their dreams and how they would achieve them. In the second group, the scientists probed about homework, about what the students thought they were doing wrong and needed to fix.

In parallel, they were brain monitored. In the brains of the students in the latter group, the fight, flight or freeze system lit up - muting other brain parts - narrowing down to what was necessary to survive. The negative emotion produced by the criticism impairs the brain's cognitive, perceptual and emotional capacity. For the students in the first group, other parts of the brain were activated, creating wellbeing, better immune systems and cognitive, perceptual and emotional openness [57].

Consider how much of your learning is impacted by the way you receive feedback and how you impact other people by the way you offer feedback. Do you reject feedback because it hurts, do you defend yourself feeling judged or do you see the opportunity to learn and grow?

The mindset of your teacher, coach or colleague is equally important. Whatever we expect from other people often becomes a self-fulfilling prophecy. When we expect good things to happen, they usually will. When we expect bad things to happen, they usually will.

Research supports that teachers' expectations regarding children's capacity drive the ability to learn and perform. When teachers were told that a student or a class were extremely bright and expected to make a quantum leap in academic performance in the year to come, the class would do so, even when they were randomly chosen from the school population at large. Provided the teacher believed the premise, the students performed at a much higher level than other students in similar classes [58].

When I tell you that I believe in you and know you can do it, you will naturally respond by doing it. The same is equally true when I expect you to not perform; chances are you won't, even when you have the capacity.

Most people are prone to speaking about what they want to change, their issues or the low quality of work and in so doing they increase the likelihood of it all to happen.

High-performing athletes serve as inspiration. They crave and benefit from very regular feedback to improve their performance, making them better – feedback often given on a daily basis by their coaches. These athletes look for motivating, challenging, supporting and direct feedback. It is a positive experience and, thus, they actively seek it. They choose coaches who believe in them.

Are you believing in your leader or coach? What do you choose to speak about and focus on? Consider the power of believing in each other as fellow human beings and as colleagues.

It's not only your coach's attitude towards you that matters – but equally your own attitude towards the topic you want to learn. Stanford studies found that kids' attitudes towards math more than their IQ determines how good they will be at math. Kids with a positive attitude towards math boosted their memory center, raising their level of math performance. Other capacities such as their IQ were found to be less relevant. The scientists were surprised to see the significance a positive attitude had on the problem-solving capabilities [11].

What you believe, you will achieve.

The mindset you hold in relation to learning is the biggest driver or limitation for what you learn. It requires daring to explore your own capacity. To slip into the role of being a beginner. To learn new behaviors from scratch. To approach your old challenges in new ways. To see your own patterns of limitation. Your confidence to a large extent defines your learning capacity. Your attitude to a large extent defines how much you will learn.

Pause, connect and reflect. How does this step – I Learn Every Day – make you think and feel?

How do you grow? Do you have a habit of blaming yourself when you fail? Or do you typically identify, share and celebrate your small, as well as your big, failures and upsets, turning them into setups for learning?

Signature Practice: Ask for Feedback

It is time to bring out your transformation journal, activating your heart and hands.

Why Ask for Feedback?

Asking for Feedback from your leader, peer, or team provides you with all of the following:

- **Inspiration.** You evolve your behaviors, making your contribution more valuable.
- **Self-awareness.** You reveal your blind-spots and increase awareness about yourself.
- **Growth.** You continuously learn from other people.
- **Trust.** You improve relationships by showing other people that their perspectives matter.

Realizing these benefits requires you to take the initiative and frequently ask for Feedback from different stakeholders including customers.

How to Ask for Feedback?

When you choose to Ask for Feedback, you benefit from being open and vulnerable, taking ownership of Your own growth and deepening your relationships.

Ask for Feedback when you are truly interested in hearing the feedback, listen deeply and engage in takingthe feedback forward into your growth.

It does not need to be complicated or take much time; ask your leaders, colleagues, customers and stakeholders.

Assist the person giving feedback by making your intention clear. For example, 'I would like you to support my growth and therefore I am asking for your feedback through two questions.'

In your eyes ...

1. What is working well?
2. What could be even better if ...?

All dimensions are important.

- **Support you.** Encourage people not to label or punish you – enabling your growth.
- **In your eyes.** Remind each other that someone's feedback is only a perspective serving you as inspiration. You decide its relevance. Do you 'let it go' or 'let it in'?
- **What is working well?** Start with the positive to make sure you hear it. We often focus on what is not good enough. Also, our strengths flourish by receiving attention.
- **What could be even better if ...?** Always ask a future-focused, yet specific question, which gives you new ideas to experiment, leaving blame and shame behind.

It takes courage, curiosity and self-compassion to Ask for Feedback.

- **Ask frequently.** Ask for Feedback frequently – ideally daily – to keep yourself learning.
- **Share your concern.** If you are concerned about the feedback you receive, share with the 'feedbacker' for them to support and care for you.
- **Small chunks.** The smallest change can make the biggest difference. Integrate small chunks, to digest. Getting overwhelmed dealing with too much is not helpful.
- **Be specific.** What exactly do you want feedback on/about?
- **Choose for growth.** Ask people who will balance support and challenge. Choose people with different perspectives – people who believe in you.
- **Say thank you.** Even if you don't agree or if the feedback was delivered in a non-constructive way, the person has invested time in your growth.

When you Ask for Feedback, you will often be asked to provide feedback to other people. Reflect on your intentions.

- Are you in the service of the other person's growth in the way you provide feedback?
- Is there a better way of giving feedback waiting for you to explore it?

Pause, connect and reflect

After using the Ask for Feedback practice for a period, cement your learnings.

The most important learning is likely to be how you respond to – rather than the actual – feedback. It often activates your triggers (amygdala), sometimes firmly, sometimes in a subtle way. Becoming aware of what is going on for you enhances your learning capacity.

- How and why do you select feedbackers? Your fans or critics?
- How does the feedback make you feel and react?
    - Do you allow yourself to truly feel the 'what is working well' part?
    - Do you receive the feedback from a mindset of fear or love?
        - Do you seek confirmation or exploration?
        - Are you defending or digesting?
        - Do you want to explain or expand?
- What is the business value of you and your colleagues regularly Asking For Feedback?

Make it a daily healthy habit and never leave a week without Asking for Feedback. The more you practice, the easier it will be to remain in a learning mindset.

Asking for Feedback is core to learning.

Being the good boy?

Implementing the Ask for Feedback as a Signature Practice in one of my workplaces, I had an extraordinary experience with Ken in my team. He had worked for the company for less than a year and jumped on the Signature Practice, asking people every day for feedback, eager to learn, or at least so it appeared.

However, when he came back to me, sharing the feedback he had received, I sensed that he sought out feedback to prove himself. He came back to me praising himself with all the good stuff, as well as how much he was living our Signature Practice. For example, he told me, 'I presented to the board. They loved what I did and wanted me to support them even further'. Ken wanted to shine in front of me and continued, 'One board member said that she had never seen anything better than this.'

I sensed his armor and fear, him not being open and relaxed. The team were annoyed by his self-promoting character and they avoided him, and I did too. As he greenwashed his stories, making them better than they were, distance was created, and people did not trust him. He did what he could to stay safe and avoid failures, thus stagnating in his growth.

When I started focusing on the process, instead of the actual feedback, with an eye on what was going on for him, progress happened: 'How did you choose people to give you feedback?' 'How was it for you to listen to the feedback?' I probed.

After a while, he saw the pattern - always choosing people who validated and praised him. He chose to collect feedback from situations where he knew he had performed well. He was on a mission to prove himself rather than to learn. He barely remembered anything that 'could be even better', since he was afraid of not being good enough, and therefore not fully trusting he would survive negative feedback. As talented as he was cognitively, his mindset did limit him.

The work for him was to celebrate how he slowly, but surely, dared to step into actively listen, being open towards feedback, acknowledging that his fear often was activated. Instead of celebrating him delivering a great presentation, we started celebrating that he had become aware of his fear. Ken had significant challenges accepting who he was (Step Two). Hence opening up towards learning happened for him very slowly and way below the pace his cognitive ability would predict.

Even though we did make progress, it did unfortunately not happen fast enough. Many relapses into old behaviors made the team neither trust nor believe in Ken, and equally, I lost my belief. We decided that ending the working relationship would be the best way forward, allowing him to start afresh in a new setting.

Could I have avoided it? I am not sure, but I took as an important learning that I could have started earlier focusing on the process of feedback rather than the output.

From Ken's experience we learn that it is often not our cognitive capacity that defines the pace of our learning, but rather our mindset that determines how much of our capacity we access and release.

From this experience what do you recognize within yourself or other people?

Creative companies outperform their peers

What does the ability to constantly learn mean to a business?

While there are many reasons why companies perform well, such as market position and technology leadership, companies that operate more creatively are consistently seen outperforming their peers, not only regarding growth, but also with respect to shareholder return. The basis for creativity is curiosity and learning – integrating feedback as a practice for learning [(59)].

We often become dependent on external consultants or a few people from the 'Transformation Office' to bring Transformational Capacity. Why? Have we avoided, missed or do not know how to build our own Transformational Capacity? Is it not a priority? When we miss the opportunity to listen, learn and act big and bold ourselves, we miss fully leveraging our human capacity.

Staying in our comfort zones is a way in which we make transformations get stuck. Staying with old behaviors, old ways of doing things can waste progress, time and money. To succeed in business transformations as individuals and institutions, we need to dare to listen, learn and act in new ways, seeing the transformation itself as an opportunity to experiment, expand and evolve – to see new opportunities (15).

Always, if you are in doubt or want to accelerate your transformation, say to yourself what you know to be true: *I have infinite capacity.*

Before we move to the next step, note down your answer to the following question in your transformation journal.

As every moment offers opportunity for learning, how is this moment a gift?

Step Seven: I Manifest Impact

'We are what we repeatedly do. Excellence, then, is not an act, but a habit.'

WILL DURANT (60)

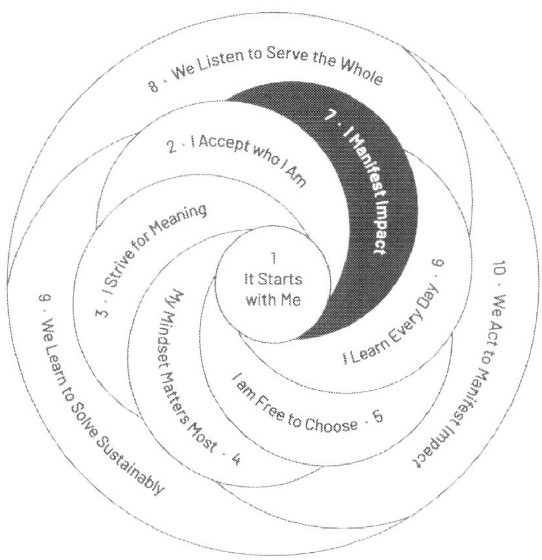

Transformations often start with excitement, and after a while there is a risk of it fizzling or fading out as people fall back to doing things they have always done. What a waste!

How have you activated and brought to life all the insights gained so far? How do you make it last – not returning to old behaviors, which is what frequently happens in transformations?

You might already have started to create value in a new way, without you being able to see it in tangible outcomes. Even though you do not see it yet, you might be able to feel it. Now, do you dare to stay the cause? When you lose your conviction, stamina or focus you are at risk of slipping back to old behaviors, adding waste rather than creating value.

Step Seven turns your insights and learnings into actions and impact. It will equip you to enhance your contribution to other people and your company – enhancing the value you create.

Dreams and discipline

You might explain: 'I read the book, but I have not yet started implementing.'

Have you said that about other insights gained from books before this one? Is it a pattern for you to look for the next book to inspire you? Even when you read with great passion and like what you read, you will not manifest impact unless you bring it into practice.

Have you ever made a New Year resolution that you did not keep? Haven't we all?

In January, the gym is full of people and diet books sell out. Fitness centers make a fortune on people's hopes and dreams, as do publishers of diet books. By February things normalize: It's back to the same familiar crowd at the gym, people who work out as a regular healthy habit regardless of New Year resolutions. Meanwhile, the latest diet book is now collecting dust on the shelf!

For you to manifest impact, for you to realize your dreams and your meaning, you need constant inspiration and discipline. Willpower is not enough to make the change happen; rather, the reward you achieve will help you make your change last.

Is your community helping you step into inspiration and disciplining you to realize your dreams? We are social creatures. Surroundings and community help or hinder us developing and keeping healthy habits. We are impacted by the communities we choose to surround ourselves with and this means we are more likely to stick to a resolution when we explicitly commit to it with someone else.

I want you to take it seriously, to build and maintain your Transformational Capacity. This, to a large extent, will define your future contribution, resourcefulness, relevance and resilience.

Working hard to perform

You might say, 'I am already exhausted; I don't know how to squeeze in more.'

You are right. Many of us are exhausted these days. Working smarter not harder is not the answer. Many of us are working in industries disrupting and going through transformations. You might feel you are working two jobs – one performing for now and one transforming for the future. Transforming is exciting and so is performing but it can feel exhausting to do both. And it is our new reality. It is not going to change.

When I talk about performing, I mean contributing as a more holistic way to look at your performance. You might think about performance as What you need to deliver by When and then working hard to achieve it. Traditional performance goals predominately capture the What, focusing on making the goals SMART (Specific, Measurable, Attainable, Realistic and Time-based)[61].

Contribution, on the other hand, combines and balances the Why, What and How of your work, aligning your goals with your company goals, capturing Why they are relevant and How you contribute – securing that you do not succeed at the expense of other people and that you have what is needed to make it happen, not wasting energy and focus. Contribution firmly moves performance from a 'me-focus' to a 'we-focus'.

Step Seven brings working smarter, not harder to the next level, focusing on how you perform optimally over time, moving from a narrow focus of performing to a broader focus of contributing. With this understanding, you will explore how you perform in today's world while transforming yourself keeping an eye to the future.

Manifest more by doing less

You might object here: 'I believe I don't have more to give!'

Let's learn from history. In October 1911, two brave men, Roald Amundsen and Robert Falcon Scott and their teams, were competing to reach the South Pole first. Scott had a bigger ship, double the budget, triple the men and several forms of transportation, including dogs, motor sledges, Siberian ponies and skies. Amundsen and his team only had one - dogs - and reached the South Pole 300 miles ahead of Scott's team!

Why did Amundsen achieve his goal while Scott and all his men died on the return from the South Pole?

Amundsen had chosen one transportation method and mastered it. With great care he selected his dogs and team, and he knew how to manage them optimally. They traveled 15 miles a day, no more as he didn't want to exhaust his team, with his end goal in mind. He did less and then obsessed. Obsession here is not meant as an addiction without balance and wellbeing but as focus and intensity.

We tend to believe that doing more is better than doing less, despite the proven impact of focus yielding much higher outcomes and contributions. That is when focus means choosing fewer priorities combined with an immense dedication in efforts towards excelling. If you don't obsess, showing up with both focus and intensity, you will only do less, which will not bring you to peak performance; only the combination of the two works.

Being overwhelmed is a real productivity killer. Business transformations often feel overwhelming because we don't prioritize; rather, we fall into the spreading-ourselves-too-thin-trap and the complexity-trap – like Scott, whose several transportation modalities added more complexity.

In companies, complexity-traps happen because of the desire for progress. We pile on goals, priorities, tasks, metrics, check points, team members and so on. We know that the Do-Less-Then-Obsess people significantly outperform the Do-More-Then-Stress people (34).

Many of us are too quick to say 'Yes'. We want to belong, want to be liked and might have been infected by FOMO (Fear Of Missing Out). Saying 'No' is uncomfortable, especially the first couple of times. Saying 'No' to one thing is saying 'Yes' to something else. High performing individuals know how to say 'No'.

If you are ever in doubt what to focus on and say 'Yes' to, connect back to your purpose and let that guide you. You will not regret your choices. With focus and intensity, you manifest impact.

Lazy, but flexible

You might be thinking, 'I have spread myself thin my whole life. How do I change that?'

Our brain is lazy. Think about your brain as an infrastructure of highways, roads, small paths and open fields. The brain prefers to use known and well-used pathways that already more or less operate as paved highways.

As long as it looks difficult to enter or unknown, the brain does not make the effort to explore new pathways that may lead to something exciting or an overall smoother journey. Our brain simply optimizes its energy spend, and exploring a new path requires more energy. Our brain is, however, flexible.

When you explicitly express that you want to take a small, untested and rustic path, your brain collaborates, until you stop paying attention, at which point it returns to the familiar paved highway.

At first this process might feel cumbersome. You need to pay attention to stay on the path, but after only 21 days the path has for many of us grown into a proper road and after an average of 66 days it is a well-functioning highway. The old highway that felt so familiar and easy has in the meantime shrunk into a more off-beaten path not being used. The brain is lazy and now defaults to the new highway [62][63].

Change made, habit established.

Building new habits sounds easy, whereas in fact it can be quite difficult. Often, we stand in the way of ourselves by building stories or excuses to justify old habits. After all, the old habits are there for a reason. They have served us well up until now. Our minds need to be challenged to see the opportunities of new habits; by checking the stories we tell ourselves and whether they remain valid.

Take a habit of mine, for example, 'I value honesty and I give straight feedback to people so they know where I stand, which will help them grow'. Is it really true? No! In fact, my habit of giving direct and straight feedback was not helpful. It was perceived as harsh, and therefore people lost their self-confidence, which was not serving their growth.

I first had to understand that what I loved giving, people did not love receiving and it was for me to accept and change. I had to slow it down to learn with practice and discipline to give feedback with the right balance of support and challenge. Compassion is to give feedback in a serving way, adjusting my How of giving feedback to achieve what I want to serve: people's growth.

'I cannot say "No"', I hear very commonly from other people. And when I ask 'Is that really true?', often it is not. The reality is that you might want to look good or be nice, which is not the same as not being able to say 'No'. In fact, saying 'No' could be a way to look even better in a few areas knowing that focus combined with intensity leads to peak performance.

We all tell ourselves stories that help us hold on to our old, potentially not so healthy habits. We have to let go of our old mindset and stories when they no longer serve us in order to replace them with new better stories, leading to healthier and more productive outcomes. We might, however, not see them as stories; we might think they are true.

What are the stories you tell yourself to keep doing what you are doing? Are they still serving you? Are they really true?

On the sofa

I entered our home, I was new in my relationship with my partner Michael and there he was lying on the sofa again. Really? 'Michael, you cannot simply lie there', I prompted with an intense voice. 'You have to do something', I continued, hovering above his head. 'I am', he quietly responded, looking me straight in the eye. 'What do you mean? What are you doing lying on the sofa? It looks like doing nothing to me!'

The truth of the matter was that Michael, after having had a strong business career as an investment banker, at the age of 41 had decided to pursue his dream of becoming a full-time triathlete with a vision of winning the national Danish championship. Being a thorough man, Michael knew that recovery was as an important part of training as swimming, biking and running. Without recovery, he would not be able to give it his best during the next hard workout.

In sport I learned from Michael and I have managed to take good care of my body in terms of what I eat and what type of training is appropriate for me. I understand that if I want to do well, I need to balance my desire to give everything with what my body can cope with. Through intense training I grow myself and my body's ability to cope with pressure and by managing both volume and intensity I avoid injuries. I balance mid- and long-term goals and my dreams of a sustainable higher level of sport performance in every training session.

Changing from sport to business clothes, I have not always been able to transfer that knowledge to my corporate world. Recovery? Breaks? Pauses? What are they? Eating during meetings and in front of the computer felt very effective.

Today, I can hear how stupid that sounds, but I firmly believed my own logic. Also, it had become a general pattern in the office – so I thought it was the right thing to do.

Until ... I signed up for wearing heart monitoring pads for a week. That week's heart data outlined – with convincing clarity – which of my habits were healthy and which were not. Whereas I was in a great shape as a sport athlete, I was challenged in terms of becoming a real corporate athlete, sustaining high performance for a long period of time, with as healthy habits in corporate life as I had in my sporting life [64].

This had implications for me but also for my team. Who was the trendsetter of this habit of eating in front of the computer, having no breaks in the office? I was! For some in my team it had therefore become challenging to take time for recovery because I did not.

As I started becoming aware, I saw the reduction in output and the pain I caused when I operated as a 'Do-more-then-stress' leader compared to when I was able to prioritize and focus – and through that create flow.

From the heart data, I was surprised to learn how recovery is different for different people. Michael recovers well on the sofa. I recover great during Check-Ins at work, connecting to myself and other people while generating focus. They help my overall wellbeing, including my sleep.

Another effective recovery method for me is watching Netflix! What a great find! Before discovering that, I felt guilty and unproductive watching marvelous series. With the new insight about my heart and health, I now celebrate my Netflix moments. Could I have known without the data? Yes, but I did not acknowledge what I knew to be true.

Consider how often you know what is good for you but don't take time to listen to yourself?

Michael knew that his heart and whole body go into great recovery lying on the sofa. As a sports athlete, Michael's competition season lasted four months. He chose to compete in only two important races per year. What about you as a corporate athlete? Are you not working every day to make a difference? Don't you want to win every single customer meeting? Are you not combining a sprint with a marathon every day?

Michael achieved his dream of becoming the Danish and European Champion several times in his age group. I learned so much from watching his tremendous discipline and attention to important details every day, all year round. Knowing what was good for him and turning them into healthy habits – many small steps towards the better every day.

From my experience with Michael, I have learned how peak performance cannot happen without balancing recovery and intensity. As I slowly but surely transfer healthy habits from the world of sport into business, I see the potential of us becoming top performing corporate athletes.

What elements in this experience do you identify with in yourself or other people?

A life of habits and intention gaps

You might reflect: 'I don't think too much about what I am doing. I go through life on autopilot.'

Most of us will recognize this picture. And the things we repeatedly do and what we spend time thinking about ultimately forms us. They become the things we believe in, and the personality we portray. They shape our lives without us noticing.

Your life is essentially the sum of your habits. How in shape or out of shape you are is a result of your habits; how happy or unhappy you are is a result of your habits; how successful or unsuccessful you think you are is a result of your habits [(65)].

Habits make up a huge proportion of our daily lives. A study of student diaries and community members indicates that up to 45 percent of daily activities and tasks we undertake are habitual. Once formed, habits become second nature and breaking or changing them difficult. Changing habits feels like a new task that can be overwhelming and a hassle in our lives. We stick with our unhealthy habits and struggle to adopt new, healthier ones. We tell ourselves stories about why we should not or cannot change [(66)].

We see this dynamic unfold in the gap between intention and action. Most of us know what is good for us; instinctively we know what healthy and unhealthy habits are and yet we fail to repeatedly acknowledge and tap into the benefits healthy habits provide. For example, most adults know that exercise is rewarding and would like to do more, yet global studies show that 36 to 55 percent of us never manage to convert intention into action.

Without feeling the immediate reward of our efforts, it is hard for us to stick to a new routine; our old and less healthy habits also provide benefits, like relaxation, connection and peace [(67)].

Companies are equally challenged by the difficulties of changing habits. We might have agreed to change and do x, but because we are used to doing y, we keep doing it. Our Say/Do ratio, reflected as our ability and reliability in executing on what we say to ourselves and other people in terms of promises, intentions, agreements and plans, thereby deteriorates.

Having a low congruence between what we think, feel and do can harm our culture and company. We trust more and feel better when our Say/Do ratio is high, ideally getting close to 1:1, and yet it is human to fall into this gap between intentions and action, making us achieve less [66].

Let's look at the Say/Do ratio as a phenomenon. Let's imagine you promise your colleague to deliver on Monday, as you know it means a lot to him, even though it will require you to work during the weekend. Neither you nor your family likes your habit of working every weekend, but you feel that you have to due to the pressure from work. You have forgotten the birthday party on Sunday, preventing you from getting work done.

The week starts full-on with endless meetings and only on Friday do you manage to deliver what you promised. During the week you feel guilty and use a fair amount of energy on explanations: 'If only my leader would not load me so much', 'Too many people invite me to too many meetings', 'We have too many private things going on during weekends'. At the end of all your arguments – ask yourself the question: 'Is that really true?'

You know that it is true you promise to deliver without having taken your own capacity and time fully into consideration and therefore you deliver late while feeling guilty. When you face and fully accept that as a pattern, you can make the healthy choices and actions to improve your reliability.

'Okay then', you might surrender, 'how do I make it a healthy habit?'

Your brain is lazy, but it is also flexible, provided you work proactively and intensively with it. Neural networks can be changed through repetition. Our brain makes up about two percent of our weight, consuming 20 percent of our energy. It requires energy to change habits; it is tiring. Your brain is constantly looking for ways to save effort, clinging on to habits that cost less energy even when they don't make sense any longer.

When you realize something is healthy to you, make it a habit! When you involve other people your success rate increases. A study on accountability found that you have a 65 percent chance of completing a goal if you commit to do it with someone else. When you feel accountable towards a person you have committed to, you will increase your chance of success by up to 95 percent [68].

It is time to find a Healthy-Habit-Buddy. Having healthy habits is not selfish; it is self-nourishing.

It takes 10,000 hours to achieve mastery and yet consistent practice will take us a little further, faster. Champions don't do extraordinary things. They do ordinary things without thinking - making it seem effortless without pain. They become masters through commitment and repeated practice [69].

For example, for Michael and me, life is simple when it comes to sport because our first question every day is: 'What exercise are we going to do today? Swimming, biking, running or gym?' It is not about 'if', only what and when. You have created a habit when the negotiation and debate stop, and the only effort is put into doing the practice.

Pause, connect and reflect. How does this step - I Manifest Impact - make you think and feel?

How do you contribute? Do you focus on What you need to deliver for you to succeed? Or are you more focused on How you contribute to other people and your company, balancing your Why, How and What? How do you assess your own overall Say/Do ratio at work and in life?

Signature Practice: Remove Your Barriers

It is time to bring out your transformation journal, activating your heart and hands.

Why Remove Your Barriers?

Often you know what is good for you, yet staying the course is difficult. You might find yourself negotiating with and explaining to yourself or other people why you are not doing what you wanted to do. As you Remove Your Barriers for execution you achieve a number of benefits leading to you creating the impact you want to.

- **Reality.** You might be dreaming of the impact you want to manifest. As you Remove Your Barriers you face your current reality, a first step for you to being able to turn your dreams into impact. Dreams can become waste if not delivered on.
- **Awareness.** As you Remove Your Barriers you will become aware of how you explain and excuse your behaviors, rationalizing events and circumstances as arguments for not having to change. Awareness is a critical foundation for creating impact.
- **Healthy Habits.** Building healthy habits will help you overcome explanations and excuses, helping you to de-risk the tendency of slipping back to old behaviors, never achieving what you wanted to.
- **Impact.** As you face your current reality, build awareness and healthy habits and keep busting your barriers by dealing with your excuses and explanations, you will be on a great path to manifesting impact.

How to Remove Your Barriers?

Be ambitious but realistic. It works when you work it. It requires discipline and inspiration.

The following dimensions will get you there a little faster:

- **Doable.** The smaller the step, the more likely you are to stick to it! One step towards better is all that is needed. Be ambitious but realistic. What is a realistic, manageable step you want to take?
- **Benefits.** Identify the benefits associated with the new habit. You give up something letting go of your old habit. Is there a fair exchange – short- and long-term – with the change of habit?
- **Plan.** It takes on average 66 days – some say 21 days – to build new pathways in your brain to build a new healthy habit. You need a specific plan. How do you plan to stick to your 21-day challenge: when, what, who, where, how much?
- **Support.** When you commit to a 21-day challenge together with another person you are more likely to establish a new healthy habit. Who will be interested and who will you enjoy doing it with? Give the person the permission to challenge you if your barriers show up and keep you to your commitment if you slide.
- **Excuses.** Your excuses, explanations and stories give you good arguments for skipping your new behaviors and habits. Excuses and stories might be your biggest barrier to bust, standing in the way of you acting and executing as you want.

Daily

Excuses give you permission not to change your behavior in order to manifest what you know is good for you and/or your company. Make it a daily healthy habit to reflect on your actions and non-actions, as well as your stories, explanations and excuses.

- How was my Say/Do ratio today?
- What stories, explanations and excuses did I tell myself today?
- Are they really true?
- What will I do tomorrow to overcome my stories, explanations and excuses?

Is it really true?

Become a barrier buster in your own and other people's lives by asking the question 'Is it really true?' when you listen to yourself and your colleagues reasoning for a slowdown in execution, low Say/Do ratio or lack of discipline, congruence and consistency. For example, 'We can't do it', 'Others will be better at this', 'We are too old for that', 'Our customers would not want that', 'We don't have time' ... and ...

Without making anything or anyone wrong, continue to ask the question, 'Is it really true?'

This is a brilliant question to explore the validity of stories that might keep everyone's current mindset active. Sometimes the stories are true even if they sound like excuses. You benefit from staying open and curious as you explore [70].

Pause, connect and reflect

After using the Remove Your Barriers practice for a period, cement your learnings.

- How are you able to overcome your excuses and barriers for execution?
- How many of the Signature Practices have you turned from insights and inspiration into healthy habits building your Transformational Capacity?
- What is the value creation for your business when you and everyone else do what you have agreed to do?

Imagine the value created by every one of us learning, loving and living the choices we have made, jointly and consistently.

Build healthy habits that remove your barriers and transform your life, exactly as you want them to.

When you work it, it works.

We like you better now, Dad

Samir was an account manager struggling in the transition from work to home. Often, he arrived at home digesting his day at work. He caught himself drifting in his thoughts at home, only brought back to the present moment by one of his children calling out to him: 'Daddy are you listening?' 'Yes', he lied, too ashamed to admit that he could not focus on his family while being with them.

His wife was the peace- and pace-maker in the house and he the order-taker, too tired and wired up to feel responsible for anything or anyone. 'Now, put the plates on the table.' 'Now, do the dishes.' 'Now, this that and the other', she would say. Endless routines.

While he removed barriers for execution and created flow at work, he was not able to bring this capacity into his private life for the benefit of him and his family. He told himself many times that a change was needed, but it never happened.

Attending a meditation training became his breakthrough. Samir learned to scan into all parts of his body in a simple five-minute breathing exercise. It helped him put aside any remaining thoughts from the day, becoming fully present in the moment first for himself and subsequently also for other people. He made a daily habit to breathe peacefully for five minutes in the car before he entered the house. His family responded united: 'We like you much more now, Daddy'.

From Samir's experience we learn how five minutes of focused (breathing) time can have a tremendous impact on us and our surroundings. Many of us hold limiting beliefs about what it means to be effective and productive. Slowing down to speed up as a way to create flow is usually not a part of our corporate habits, despite research illustrating the positive impact conscious breathing and meditation have on our brain capacity and energy levels [71].

I recognize myself so much in Samir when I am not present and I want to be, and how much energy I waste in pretending that I am present, instead of using the energy to create conditions for me to be present. How complicated we make life for ourselves. What in Samir's story resonates with you?

Transformations lacking relentless execution

Can we transfer knowledge about how to drive individual peak performance to institutions?

Yes. When we take a more holistic approach to performance than we often do, considering both the performance and the health of our company we outperform our peers. Organizational performance is What a company delivers in terms of improved financial and operational results for its stakeholders measured through metrics, including revenue, profit, cost and return on capital.

Organizational health is How effective people work together to pursue their common goal – evaluated through the level of internal alignment, quality of execution and capacity to renew themselves to sustain high performance in an ever-changing external environment [72].

Fifteen years of research confirm that as a company we can reach higher performance when we balance and integrate organizational performance and health, focusing equally on the What (hard) and the How (soft) aspects.

There are numerous examples of successful organizations who understand the importance of achieving the balance and integration. Unfortunately there are countless examples of less successful organizations focusing only on short-term and performance, using the excuse, 'When we have time, we will focus on the soft stuff.' How is your company operating? And what about you?

Leaving out the soft stuff can make you survive short-term as a company, yet it is not a sustainable solution for creating long-term value. Putting equal emphasis on the What and How elements of leading change more than doubles the odds of success [73].

Many business transformations are not fading or failing because of lack of awareness, insight or choices. They fail because of lack of relentless execution. They fail because we lack perseverance when we face headwind, we get in doubt or we decide not to put in the effort – consciously or unconsciously – to manifest the impact we came for.

Instead we give up or give in and return to old habits or leave our challenges unsolved. We choose what seems a known and safe path or we simply slide into convenience, complacency and/or sloppiness. For a company this can be the detour it cannot afford. There is one question we benefit from asking ourselves: 'If it was my company, would I tolerate the safe path as an option?'

Knowing the power of Signature Practices, we have implemented them in the last companies I have worked for. They are easy to understand and simple to do, inviting the full organization to adopt them. None of the practices take more than 5-10 minutes, which removes the most obvious excuse of 'We don't have time', lowering barriers to implementation and impact.

Always, if you are in doubt or want to accelerate your transformation, say to yourself what you know to be true: *What I attend, I attract.*

Before we move to the next step, note down your answer to the following question in your transformation journal.

For me to be at my best, what are my healthy habits?

PART III

Transform Your Business

Human transformation enables business transformation

'The success of an intervention depends on the interior conditions of the intervener.'

BILL O' BRIEN [74]

In the following three – final – steps you move from focusing on your individual work of transforming yourself - already benefitting your business - to the collective work of transforming your business, together with your colleagues. You are ready to expand your ripple and raise your impact through the Transformational Capacity you have built. Your view through the lens of love also makes you look differently at organizations.

Living, breathing organisms

Most of us are used to seeing companies as machines to be optimized for making money – created, controlled and changed by their operators. Through this lens we see hierarchies, departments, goals, infrastructure, policies measurements, management decisions and governance. Companies operated as machines are likely to have a shorter life expectancy than their true potential, as this mindset does not support constant adaptation, evolution and growth[75].

When we look at an organization as a machine, we tend to focus on its parts, not the totality. We measure departments on their output, not their contribution to the whole. We tolerate politics, sub-optimization and even internal fights. It is a field of constrains, a system of fear.

I was excited to learn from Daniel Katz and Robert Kahn to view organizations not as machines but as living, breathing organisms. The two American psychologists produced the first pioneering work back in the 1960s that viewed organizations as complex, adaptive systems - offering alternative perspectives into how we lead and how we solve in these complex environments. Following their path, when we view through the lens of love, we start seeing organizations as organisms that live and breathe, we understand they create their own purpose, way of working and businesses processes. They set their own goals and actions in exchange with their surroundings, constantly adapting, evolving, growing and eventually dying like any other organism [76].

When we see companies as a living organism, we emphasize health and fair and balanced exchange with our surroundings. We look for patterns as to where things flow, flourish and function and we search for synergies - also externally - to create conditions to thrive. We want to sense the vitality of our organization and focus on removing what blocks our potential, constantly nurturing our learning, adaptation, evolution and growth. One big system living and growing together as a whole [77][78].

Do you sense what a difference it makes how you choose to view and create value in your organization?

In the human body, it is the capillaries - the finest, thinnest and by far the longest parts of our blood vessels - that are responsible for the exchange with the cells and tissues in the body, bringing them oxygen, which allows them to live, while taking away the waste of carbon dioxide so they can function optimally.

Without capillaries we could not make that life sustaining exchange happen. Similarly, the life of a company cannot be sustained and enriched without every one of us mobilized in the transformation and operating in unity. Only when we - the capillaries of our business body - consistently turn waste into value for our organizations - living the Ten Steps of Transformation - will our businesses live and breathe to their full capacity. The essence of life for both human beings and businesses.

All parts of the body work seamlessly together, each focusing on their part to keep us alive, flourishing and functioning. When a challenge occurs, such as illness, the body pulls together in collaboration to remove anything preventing the body from flowing optimally.

All parts of the body focus on what needs to be done, each part providing its contribution to restore balance – returning to strength and health. No one is waiting for anyone or any central decision to be made. All parts of the body know what is needed now. The body constantly and seamlessly allocates its resources to the parts that need it most. Always looking for health of the totality; the full body. All parts move in synchronicity, each part belonging and knowing its place.

As human beings we live with great interdependence and exchange and flow with our surroundings; trees clean the air for human beings. As human beings we inhale oxygen and exhale carbon dioxide. Leaves and plants do the opposite.

Seeing organizations as living organisms, we understand how much health and fair and balanced exchange with our surroundings matters for the value we create and how long we live. We see businesses living in fair exchange with their surroundings contributing to the societies they are part of.

As businesses we 'inhale' infrastructure, people, partnerships and raw materials and we exhale products and services for our customers and inspire people to become better sisters, brothers, friends and citizens as part of working within our businesses. Our human transformation enables both business and social transformation.

We breathe with society – our customers, our partners, the community we are part of – in a fair exchange, constantly flowing like inhaling and exhaling. We leave people, customers and all stakeholders better with each interaction, engagement by engagement, conversation by conversation, exchange by exchange. Love becomes a way of being.

Let's explore this in the next three steps.

Step Eight: We Listen to Serve the Whole

'There is a lot of difference between listening and hearing.'

G.K. CHESTERTON (79)

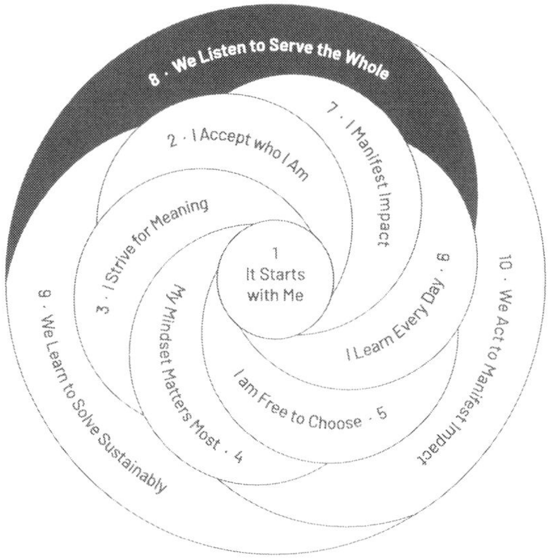

It is time for you to intensify the transformation of your business with the knowledge, wisdom, healthy habits and Transformational Capacity you have acquired so far via the first seven steps. In Step Eight, you walk the first step in solving the business challenges that keep you awake at night.

You don't step into immediate action, fixing the problem, like you might have a bias for. Rather, you take the time to understand the essence of your challenge, by deeply listening to various important voices and stakeholders: listening to the whole.

Slowing down at first prevents you from wasting any time, energy or any other resources chasing things less relevant and critical. You want to listen to the whole, understanding your various stakeholders to create a balanced and aligned focus.

This aligned focus enables you to move with accelerated speed later on as you solve challenges at their real root cause - sustainably.

Step Eight supports you to open your mind and heart, understanding where the world is heading and what it wants from you, your work and your organization. Allowing the emergence of how you can progress yourself, your organization and society with an aligned focus - listening to the whole.

Listening deeply

You might say: 'I know how to listen'.

Listening sounds simple. It is not. It is one of the hardest skills to learn - an acquired art, not an inherited capacity. When acquired, it does wonders. It allows you to see what things are and want to become, rather than what you assume, truly expanding your perspective and realm of possibilities.

Listening is not the same as hearing. Hearing is passive, whereas listening is active, a conscious effort to listen also beyond the words. Some people say that only a small percentage of what we communicate is spoken words. The rest is our energy, tone of voice and non-verbal communication [(80)].

Genuinely listening requires switching on all our senses, stepping out of being self-centered into full openness and curiosity, where you listen, connect and bridge. It requires you to suspend already familiar conceptions, beliefs and understandings. Listening skills require focus, awareness and training [(81)].

Where it is possible to talk too much, it is not possible to listen too much. The path to other people's hearts often comes through listening. To listen is to learn, a critical step in reinventing both human beings and businesses.

Have you ever enjoyed listening to talented jazz musicians improvising? They have nothing pre-prepared and play by listening to their co-players and audience. They follow the familiar structure of the song, aware of where they and the other musicians are in flow. They listen to what might come newly, spontaneously and originally to them.

Have you ever listened to someone sensing what comes next, not because it is your uncle's same old story and you know it inside out, but because you have tuned into becoming one with the person speaking? In this place, you can learn something completely new. You tap into seeing the world differently. This quality of listening we call 'deep listening'. When we enter the land of love and listen to learn, where we are open to what comes, we are listening deeply. When we enter the field of fear, we listen to protect, ready to defend our viewpoints at any point of time.

Successful organizations, leaders and people listen deeply and allow their view of the world to be challenged, exactly as Uber challenged the status quo of taxi transportation, Airbnb challenged accommodation and Netflix challenged home entertainment.

All three companies put aside usual conventions, assumptions and predefined views of the world. Instead, they listened to and sensed new patterns from the market, turning their insight into new operating models that successfully disrupted these industries.

We will all face disruption – no matter what industry – often operating in situations where the end state of our business cannot be clearly defined. We face global shifts in digitalization, robotics, artificial intelligence, the Internet of Things and regulations.

In addition come ever-increasing and evolving expectations from society as to the role of companies expecting them to have purposes with a balanced focus beyond optimizing only for the company. We can choose to resent, resist or reject the change or we can welcome the disruptions and even shape and lead them, seeking to understand by deep listening to the whole.

The rules of the game are clear: Change or be (ex)changed. What do you choose?

Purpose balancing people, profit and planet

You might counter argue: 'We don't have a purpose and we are doing fine.'

Today maybe. But what about tomorrow? Both the customer and the talent marketplace have high expectations for companies. Gone are the days where a simplistic focus on financial yield satisfying shareholders and the market is enough. As citizens and society, we are increasingly expecting companies to address pressing social and economic issues. We want organizations to have a genuine purpose and a balanced focus, with society's best interests at heart.

More and more people expect companies and the people working there to be guided by a purpose that balances the triple bottom line: people, profit and planet. Doing well and doing good. As companies we struggle to adapt when we see them as competing priorities. More and more organizations welcome it as an opportunity to align around a greater purpose. Some companies take it further as they deliberately choose to do well *by* doing good [(82)].

There is a growing opinion among thought leaders that no company without a sense of purpose can realize its full potential. Companies without a clear purpose will lose their license to operate from key stakeholders. Balancing the need of all stakeholders is critical for driving long-term sustainable growth [(83)].

How are you and your company operating today?

To create real transformation, you have to look closely at how you operate, including your blind spots, biases and assumptions. Similar to human beings (Step Two) businesses cannot transform without a defenseless calibration of reality.

Listening deeply to the whole is a paramount step in expanding your level of consciousness - your awareness of what is going on right now. You get inspired to identify what you might need to let go of, for example, a win-lose mindset that always creates waste for the totality. And give space to other things that you let come, for example, a win-win-win mindset that creates value for all.

Successful transformation, in its purpose, needs to authentically balance multiple dimensions including short- and long-term goals, transforming while performing and balancing the interests of stakeholders and shareholders. Purpose-guided businesses significantly enhance financial returns while also benefitting from having stronger trust among stakeholders, deeper customer understanding and leaner teams focusing on value creation, not sub-optimization. They have higher employee engagement and a low level of employee turnover [(21)].

What's not to like? Really, nothing. Yet it requires that we hold a mindset of love, patience and trust, everyone being guided by our purpose, knowing that a shareholders' win does not require a loss for other stakeholders.

Do you believe that when someone wins, you lose?

To listen or not to listen

You might argue: 'It takes time to listen, and very little comes out of it.' It is a time investment for sure. Sustainable transformations start by listening to and sensing your stakeholders. What are their known and unknown needs? What are they expecting from you? How do they want you to serve?

You need to slow down to speed up. This process felt uncomfortable for me the first couple of times. I was biased toward actions and wanted to jump straight into problem solving, often leading to significant waste because I did not address the root cause of the challenge. I lost speed and effort.

The German lecturer Otto Scharmer from MIT Management Sloan School inspired me with his change management/transformation method called the U-theory. He introduces a new way of listening, learning and acting in businesses – allowing teams and organizations to see new perspectives, to co-create solutions for the future, serving all stakeholders in an aligned and balanced way in a highly volatile, uncertain, complex and ambiguous world (15).

Scharmer genuinely advocates that there is no business transformation without a human transformation. When we move from an ego mindset (fear-based) to an eco-system mindset (love-based) as individuals and as businesses we are able do well and do good simultaneously.

To detect if you are really listening, ask yourself whether you are listening to judge – 'I know best!' – to prove yourself – 'See what I said!' – or to understand – 'What is needed now?'

Listening to the past: honoring the past

Have you ever listened to the past, the present and the future?

To fully understand what is needed now, you need to listen to the past. You honor and acknowledge it, which allows you to move on to the present and the future. You learn from the past and assess what rightfully should stay, go and grow. You honor that everyone and everything has a time and a place. All that has happened up until now has served and made you and your organization what it is today (84).

In a large technology company where I worked, we were too eager to force the future too fast. 'Let's go!' we called out. We wanted people to work together across the value chain in self-organizing multi-functional teams, solving problems together quickly with the customers. We wanted to bring a higher level of value to the customers fast.

Our impatient push away from where we were created a counter reaction in the organization where people were yearning towards the past, arguing how good it was back then, resisting the change. Some of us, myself included, were so preoccupied, looking and moving forward seeing all the opportunities ahead, that we neglected the road we and our organization had traveled to get here.

We became infatuated with the future and forgot to respect people, programs and products, those that came before and their contribution. People compensated by telling the missing story even louder, staying loyal to the past and bringing back the torn-out pages. Resistance, at its roots, is seldom about people reacting against what is coming but people reacting with loyalty to what was [85].

What was out of sight for a lot of us was still taking up a lot of energy and mind space for others. It kept us from collectively moving forward with full capacity. Human energy, effort and engagement were being wasted.

Divided into two unproductive counterforces, one forcing the future and one yearning for the past, we were not connecting but rather judging and blaming each other, ganging up with like-minded people against those with a different perspective.

This changed as soon as we started honoring and appreciating people for their contribution as part of our journey. We shared positive stories about how in the past we had brought value to customers - great stories about the entrepreneurial qualities of our founders enabling us to become who we were today. Even newly-arrived employees became proud of our history.

We acknowledged that there is a place and time for everything and everyone, and everyone has the right to belong. As people felt respected, those staying, those leaving and those who had already left, the organization settled and opened up to the new.

When we gave up the internal fight, we meet in the only place you can meet: in the present and in our current reality.

How are you listening to the past?

Listening to the present: calibrating current reality

To fully understand what is needed now, you need to listen to the present, helping you to calibrate and accept your current reality (Step Two). In doing so, much becomes available to you. I joined a multi-national company with low customer satisfaction and a historically high number of customers leaving the company.

When speaking to our front-line people, they explained and complained that we did not have the right products and prices to compete in the marketplace. Much effort had already been expended improving these pain points.

Only when we started systematically to listen deeply to our customers and their complaints did we understand that 70 percent of all the complaints were related to the attitude of our people when our customers were in contact with our company. Customers did not find us kind, caring, informative or reliable enough. Consequently, they did not feel seen, listened to and valued. Not surprisingly, many chose different companies to serve them.

We did not have a product problem. We operated from a mindset of Prisoners (Step Four). It was tempting to blame our front-line people, yet it turned out that it was not lack of care or passion for our customers, but rather a result of the objectives we had put in place many years ago to drive operational excellence. Those well-intended targets, such as number of calls, minutes spent with customers, time spent on preparation and idle time, had unintended consequences in terms of how our people were engaging with our customers.

We decided to remove these objectives and gave people one hour of training in deep listening. Thereafter people were fully empowered to make the decisions needed in how to serve the customers with only one requirement: to live our organizational values of ownership and courage.

Within a few months both customer satisfaction and employee engagement scores increased. When our people engaged with our customers, listening deeply, they understood what customers really wanted. Our people combined their heads, hearts and hands to deliver those solutions to our customers. Listening to our people and them listening to our customers was the needed recipe for success. This simple but impactful change made our people feel valued and appreciated.

How are you listening to the present?

Listening to the future: co-creating our future

To fully understand what is needed now, you also need to listen to the future. You do that by curiously watching out for emerging patterns, new needs being expressed, behaviors changing. It is a subtle way of listening as needs are often not expressed so clearly. You engage in the attitudes and emotional responses of the people you are listening to, setting aside your own preconceptions, prepared to embrace the thinking and viewpoint of others. You listen with all your senses to what is said and not said [(15)].

When LEDs entered the scene in the lighting industry, not much had happened for almost 20 years, with the same three big players that had been competing forever. With LED-technology suddenly everyone could produce light and the small size of the light source made it possible to apply light to very different shapes, forms and functionalities.

Working for one of the older, big players in the industry, I had the privilege to join one of our lighting designers at a global lighting fair in Germany. Here, I truly understood what listening to the future meant.

Whereas many participants at the conference skipped the small Chinese producers with the argument that that their quality was too low, our lighting designer chose to stop at their exhibition stands listening to them. How did they see the market evolving? What did they imagine could be the application potential for light in the future? He stayed open and curious, not rejecting any of the thoughts they were sharing.

I was surprised to see how much the Chinese producers shared to what potentially could be seen as a competitor. In return for his great listening skills, our lighting designer was given loads of information and ideas from the Chinese producers with grace and gratitude - for the interest shown.

A market analysis so different from the usual studies of market trends. We saw how light can be used as light, as mood and ambience creator, as artwork, as healing and wellbeing, as an alarm, as clothes fashion, as safety, as sustainability enhancer ... endless forms and functionalities.

When listening to multiple voices with different views covering the past, present and future, you much better understand the starting point of your challenge, where you come from and where you might be going.

How are you listening to the future?

Pulled by purpose

Ahead of joining a big company within the financial services industry, I attended a call with 20 people from the company where one of my colleagues-to-be in the executive team said, 'But we are not putting a man on the moon. We are just a boring bank. I am not sure that we can do anything about our culture, and do we really need a purpose and values ...?'

I remember thinking, 'Hmmm, on the face of it, I don't agree'. Yet it sparked curiosity in me. If our senior leaders feel that way, how is it for people in the organization? From my conversations I knew that the CEO, my boss-to-be, David, wanted it differently.

He knew the industry as a whole had deep problems in terms of credibility towards society. He had ambitions of a bigger existence for the bank and yet the bank was in the news almost every day, being bashed for its way of operating, accused of not having the right values. Public opinion was against us and people had to defend working for us on a daily basis.

David had listened deeply to the different voices from many stakeholders, including shareholders, as well as his own voice. He wanted to reinvent banking from a moral and ethical perspective. The bank had gone relatively untouched through the financial crisis and now believing it could walk on water. Arrogance and complacency had sneaked in. David passionately spoke to me about how we needed a change in culture, answering 'How do we become the trusted bank our customers and society want us to be?'

David was admirably transparent and honest. He knew there was much he did not know. He knew that what had brought him and the company here would not take them to where he wanted to go. He was curious and open towards something different for the bank and for the industry. I was intrigued and inspired by his humility, his burning desire, his bravery and curiosity and his trust in me as he said: 'I don't know how to do this. Do you want to help us?' How could I not?

During the first few weeks, I met with and listened to people from across the company who told me we were traveling in the 'middle of the road' and people were working in silos. 'This is our company, this is how it works', people said, nodding as if it was a given and not possible to change.

Cautious and somewhat frightened by all the negative media attention, they were not feeling proud of who they were working for. I also found much passion for the customers, and I sensed people with big hearts, yet not fully activated at work where fear was the dominant emotion showing up in many conversations.

'Wow!' I shared with David. 'What a potential to unlock when we manage to mobilize our people fully with heads, hands and hearts.' He nodded.

Two weeks later, I presented my findings to colleagues in the top team where everyone signed up for what became the very essential and unique design principle of our transformation, namely, 'There is no business transformation without a human transformation'. During the meeting we understood that it started with us. Many dimensions of the bank were not functioning optimally.

So far, we and others had been talking about it as 'them' and 'the system' as if the company was not us. The first step was to realize that if we did not transform, the company would not either. It was a challenging moment to lay down our defenses and accept who we were. And as a collective to realize that if we did not act now, we would let our organization down. We had to let go of old beliefs, outdated assumptions and behaviors fit for the past. For example, 'I deliver to the company by managing my shop' and 'If I don't challenge you, you will leave me alone to do my thing.'

These beliefs were voices of fear, which had served us in the past and kept us safe through the financial crisis, but they represented a risk-aversity that no longer fitted. It was consuming too much of our time, energy and effort. We talked about the business potential moving from fear to love. I guess it was the first time 'love' was discussed in the boardroom and maybe in any bank for that matter! Some colleagues were hesitant about the idea, feeling it was counter-intuitive, but many were excited about the opportunity.

As a team we chose to explore this path. As we, in that boardroom, recognized that we did not have all the answers we had to let go of our desire to explain or defend. We had to step out of our self-centeredness as we chose to listen deeply to our people, to our customers and our partners.

Through surveys, dialogues and many variations of smaller and bigger forums we listened deeply to and co-created with more than 7,000 of our colleagues - not assuming that we had the answers. Our people told us the following as to how we operated at that point of time.

The most often used sentence was 'Be careful' and other statements indicating fear of not being safe.

- Avoid taking ownership
- Do not question a decision or be outspoken
- Monitor rather than trust

Another typical statement was 'Avoid conflict' and similar phrases indicating fear of not belonging.

- Avoid difficult decisions
- Say Yes to everything
- Tolerate bad behavior

The third typical statement was 'Look Good' and similar phrases indicating fear of not feeling good enough.

- Hide red flags, greenwash achievements, blame and judge others
- Focus on own needs instead of customer's needs
- Make sure that my unit succeeds rather than helping others

As a leadership team we had a real 'Oh s...' moment digesting the input our people had shared. We knew that we together with our colleagues in the company had created this culture. No wonder the company had challenges in both performing and solving our more complex problems. By listening to our people, we understood what hindered progress.

All this valuable insight was gained through listening deeply. Our people had made it impressively clear what was holding us back - why we were stuck and what we needed to let go of collectively, as well as what we needed to embrace to co-create our future. When we asked ourselves if we had known, the answer was 'Yes! Deep down we knew!'

The important question was: Why we had not done anything about it? Why had we not been listening? I guess the answer is familiar to all of us. We did not fully want to know. We did not want to face the music (Step Two). Instead we buried ourselves in daily actions and operations, one day following the next without taking the time to listen to our people, to pause, connect and reflect.

Our people made it obvious to us that they missed direction and a joined focus and the bigger Why of banking and, therefore, the bigger Why of our bank. They wanted something much more profound and balanced than being another boring bank to really excite them, our customers and society at large. David and our leadership team listened and understood the need.

7,000 people contributed to developing our new shared purpose that exactly expressed that greater meaning, perspective, contribution and responsibility. This was the result:

'Together we lead the way
enabling
dreams and everyday aspirations
for
a greater good.'

♥

Wow! No word about being a bank. A purpose rooted in our societal values (together); a purpose really setting a new ambition not operating from the middle of the road (leading the way); a purpose seeing the customers as human beings (dreams and everyday aspirations) and very prominently understanding our role in society beyond our shareholders (a greater good). A pumping heart symbolizing the essence of what our people really wanted.

They wanted us to move from being self-centered to serving the whole. They wanted us to move from ego to eco. How did they know? Many of them had listened to their customers, their families and society at large. From that listening they knew something new was needed - especially that society was expecting much more from us [15].

We developed our four meter in diameter Culture Carpet capturing our new purpose and values that people could meet and stand on. This Culture Carpet became the physical manifestation of what our culture transformation was all about, capturing the kind of bank and business that we wanted to become; our greater meaning.

One beautiful morning in May we went live. 'May I introduce to you our new purpose and values?' leaders wearing T-shirts greeted and invited their colleagues in all countries, at all offices and branches to stand on the carpet for the first time. We were met with varying levels of excitement, some skeptical – not ready for hearts and hugs and wondering if the company leadership had gone mad. However, the majority of people opened their arms and hearts. Overall, it was a magical experience marking a real change.

In the next three months, our 30,000 people were invited to and participated in conversations on the carpet in smaller groupings connecting to our new purpose and values – our culture to be. We shared with each other what energized us with the new purpose and values, where we saw ourselves contributing already and where each of us had gaps to close.

We placed the carpet in all offices. We stood on it and engaged with it in all town hall meetings and big gatherings. It became our corporate fireplace.

At that time, employee engagement had never been lower in the world, particularly in the financial sector due to the constant critique and increased demands coming from society, the media and regulators. People were more exhausted than excited in our bank [4].

We worked diligently with our leaders, moving from command and control into being servant leaders embracing empowerment, combined with accountability. Engagement improved significantly, with people connecting to our new values and purpose. People felt seen, listened to and valued.

The process became a big lesson to me at so many levels. As the process owner, for the first time in my life I fully surrendered to the collective wisdom, the mighty many, not assuming that I knew how to do it. When I and other leaders trusted the process without micromanaging our people, we stepped into co-creation and things started to flow, flourish and function. We started to operate like an organism - a well-functioning body with the desire to grow.

What elements in my experience do you identify with in yourself or in your company?

Listen at your best

You might question: 'Is listening really that difficult?'

Yes, listening is a difficult skill to obtain and yet so worth it, being an incredible valuable skill.

In one study, 112 undergraduates were paired with a person instructed to be a distracted listener or instructed to listen as you listen when you are at your best. The undergraduates were asked to talk for 10 minutes about their attitude towards a particular subject. Speakers paired with good listeners (versus those with distracted listeners) felt less anxious and more self-aware, with higher clarity about their subject and were more likely to share their attitude with other people [(86)].

We all know the uncomfortable experience of sharing with someone not fully paying attention and listening.

In another study, 114 undergraduates were asked to speak for 12 minutes about their fitness for becoming a manager in the future. Speakers who spoke with good listeners were found to be more nuanced when sharing both their strengths and weaknesses in relation to becoming a manager. Meanwhile, speakers paired with poor listeners found themselves most suitable for becoming a manager. Listening simply supports us in getting more perspectives and becoming more nuanced.

When listening to people genuinely, we are likely to become more productive as we, via our listening, help other people to become psychologically safe and less defensive. Good listeners generate more trust and creativity in others. Being listened to makes us more relaxed, more self-aware and more willing to reflect in a non-self-defending manner. Listening enables us to collaborate and connect. Through our listening we can help people change [86].

Pause, connect and reflect. How does this step - We Listen to Serve the Whole - make you think and feel?

Is your habit saying: 'I know this! Let me share!' Or are you more likely to say: 'I am curious to listen ...?' or 'I wonder what is needed now ...?' By listening, I understand. By listening, I learn. By listening I balance.

Signature Practice: Listen Deeply

It is time to bring out your transformation journal, activating your heart and hands.

Why Listen Deeply?

Listening Deeply is a critical capacity to build as part of your Transformational Capacity.

- **Understanding.** You listen to understand and learn what is needed now.
- **Balanced focus.** When you Listen Deeply you gain multiple perspectives, helping you create a balanced focus.
- **Solutions.** To solve the complex challenges that keep you awake at night you need to Listen Deeply to understand. This is likely differently to how you have listened so far.
- **Relationships.** By Listening Deeply, you build relationships, understanding people and entities at a deeper level.

This practice builds on the Signature Practice 'Ask for Feedback' (Step Six) and requires the same capacity of staying open, curious and humble.

How to Listen Deeply?

There are two ways of listening:

- **Listening to protect – rooted in fear**
  You listen to judge: 'I know best!' or to be confirmed: 'See what I said!' anchored in a mindset of, often unconscious, fear.
- **Listening to learn – rooted in love**
  You listen to understand: 'What is needed now?' anchored in a mindset of love.

Listen to protect

- **Basic habitual way of listening** – reconfirms old opinions and judgments
- **Seeking confirmation** of current opinion, which is therefore likely not to change
- **Listening only to the past** – confirming preconceived ideas taking in nothing new
- **Focused on yourself** not the other person
- **Focus on debating**, to negotiate, to persuade and less to understand

Notice in which situations you are listening from a place of protection?

Listen to learn

- **Full attention** and creating an emotional connection to the person speaking.
- **Seeing the world** and situation through their eyes.
- **Understanding the person** at a deeper level, including their needs.
- **Listen to the future** by sensing what could become possible.
- **Gaining greater awareness** of individuals and situations.
- **Focus on what is said and not said**, as well as body language and tone of voice.

Notice in which situations you are listening from a place of learning?

Listening in a new way to your stakeholders

- **Complex issues** are best solved when you get a 360-degree perspective in terms of insight and inspiration on the matter. Avoid wasting time and effort on quick fixes – rather look for the root cause.
- **Select two to three relevant diverse stakeholders** to listen to.
- **Include important stakeholders you serve** to gain a fresh perspective on the challenges that keep you awake at night.
- **Set up undisturbed quality time** with each stakeholder.
- **Explain your intent**, including practicing the new skill of Listen Deeply, not debating.
- **Stay open** to what might emerge, identifying known and unknown needs – taking you and your stakeholder to places you have not been before to openly explore.

Listening, the secret source to connection

- **Full attention.** Give your 100 percent attention with eye contact.
- **New insight.** Do not interrupt and you will gain new insight.
- **Stay open.** Do not impose your solutions – stay open.
- **Open questions.** Continue to ask open questions.

There are two questions to ask and for you to profoundly understand – when listening to your stakeholders.

1. How does success look to you?
2. How can I be of great(er) service to you and what we together create?

Don't stop the Listen Deeply practice here. Think about all your relationships, established or not yet established, as your stakeholders wanting to be listened to in a deep way.

You can gain further insight by adding the two questions from the Signature Practice 'Ask for Feedback' (Step Six).

3. In your eyes – what works well?
4. What could be even better if ...?

Pause, connect and reflect

After using the Listen Deeply practice for a period, cement your learnings.

- How is it for you to listen? Do you manage to stay quiet, humble, curious and patient?
- How do you manage to connect to your stakeholders and their needs?
- What new insight, learnings and possibilities do you sense and gain?
- Who did you select as your stakeholders and who are you not listening to?
- How does listening deeply to stakeholders impact your work and your business?

The more you practice, the better you will become. Make it a daily practice to Listen Deeply to someone who matters to you, or someone you did not think mattered to you. You may be surprised when you start listening.

Enjoy the wonders of listening!

A question that deserves a question

In all the companies I've worked for, listening has been a challenge, especially for leaders. Many of us desire to take command, direct conversations, talk more rather than listen. We demand ourselves to have the answers, and are often recruited to leadership positions as experts, expected to possess relevant knowledge. Yet having all the answers does not allow us to shine a light on our people, nor facilitate growth by supporting them in finding the answers.

In one company, we implemented Coffee Corners as a practice for informal gatherings and as an action to enhance our individual and organizational listening capacity. People from all parts of the organization voluntarily met our leaders to have a dialogue for an hour. The rules of a Coffee Corner are simple. The topic is decided by the people showing up. The leader facilitates the dialogue by asking questions rather than answering questions. People can change the subject and are free to join or leave whenever they wish, based on their interest in the dialogue.

At the beginning, everyone struggled with the format. It felt unusual and almost too unstructured to relate to in a workplace. I remember how Simon, leading a big part of our sales organization, had to deal with his preconceived ideas about himself. He thought he was supposed to be interesting and have good answers, thinking about what he was going to say rather than listening to what people were sharing. The Coffee Corners became a great learning platform for him.

'Why are we not achieving our targets for online meetings with our customers?' a person from marketing asked in one of the Coffee Corners. His frowning face and critical voice tempted Simon to jump into answering, based on a recent discussion from a leadership team meeting. He stopped himself, instead returning the question: 'I am really not sure. Would you have any reflections yourself?'

The person hesitated but answered: 'Our recent survey shows that our customers enjoy online meetings as they can call in from home at their convenience; thus it's effective for them. Our people, however, like customers to come to the office as they are not so familiar with how the online meetings run. Our salespeople feel they connect better with customers when they are in the same room. So, how's that for customer service?' he asked, beaming.

This statement was followed by silence in the group, people clearly trying to absorb what had been made very transparent. Several salespeople were present, and the atmosphere was tense for a while, until one guy leaned forward: 'Honestly, I don't ask my customers what they want. I assume they want the same as me. Physical meetings are convenient to me. It means that I have time for fewer meetings as they typically take longer. I don't want to be pushed into having more meetings with more customers in one day. I realize that I have made it convenient for me not for my customers.'

There was silence; everyone digesting. Simon's next question was warmly asked and powerful: 'Anyone operating in a similar way?' A honest show of hands went up. We had accepted reality – together – as it was (Step Two), prioritizing our convenience over customer service. Now we could do something about it.

All this insight was new to Simon as it became apparent that we in the leadership team had not really understood the problem. The real impact of the conversation was, however, the engagement and desire to do something about the problem, created among those people attending the Coffee Corner.

Simon celebrated people's courage, their honesty and ability to find solutions going forward, benefitting the customers. He equally came to appreciate that it was alright not having all the answers, not seeing this as his incompetence. His acceptance allowed him and the company to listen and learn all we needed to understand from our great people.

From Simon's experience, we learn how easy it is to assume we know what our customers or any other relationships want from us, without asking them.

What do you recognize in this experience in you or other people?

Listening to the whole

History is full of examples of individuals, teams and companies not listening and thereby getting into trouble. History is equally full of examples of companies in deep trouble making a turnaround by listening to their stakeholders. For example, Dell had the worst customer satisfaction and managed to leap to the best. Dell's solution was that it changed its culture and customer service practice, including making big strides to genuinely connect with customers, understanding their needs. The business made big improvements by staying open to feedback and putting listening at the heart of running the business.

Many business transformations lack listening to what is really needed and therefore they lack a balanced focus and prioritization in the midst of often delivering on an ambitious agenda: 'Do you want customer satisfaction or a reduction in cost?' people ask. There is only one answer: 'We want both'.

When we are overwhelmed, we try to make life simplistic when it is not. We like 'either that or this'. The polarities calm us down. Yet it is an illusion as our world is complex with many dilemmas and trade-offs. We need to listen to establish an aligned focus.

Transformations mean doing things differently, including embracing the 'both/and' and the healthy tension of listening to and serving multiple stakeholders. There is no purpose without profit and there will be no long-term profit without purpose. Our inability to integrate and create win-win-win solutions makes us swing the pendulum from one extreme, often followed closely by a swing to another extreme – wasting resources in time, cost, energy and effort.

Through our lens of fear, it looks like contradicting and conflicting forces pulling in different directions. Through our lens of love, we see and understand them as healthy tensions that allow us to breathe as a business - welcoming the constant disruption and enrichment tensions offer.

Well-known companies illustrate that businesses can do well by doing good, listening to and serving all stakeholders, as, for example, Whole Food Markets, Southwest Airlines, Google, Patagonia and more do. To create value for all major stakeholders requires strong listening skills, trust, compassion, collaboration - all capacities reflecting a mindset of love holding a perspective of 'we and the totality' contrary to the limiting view of 'me and mine' [(87)].

Always, if you are in doubt or want to accelerate your transformation, say to yourself what you know to be true: *Everyone and everything belongs and serves. Past, present and future.*

Before we move to the next step, note down your answer to the following question in your transformation journal.

As we seek to understand, how are you listening?

Step Nine: We Learn to Solve Sustainably

'The challenges in organizations start with the frenetic pace many people feel compelled to maintain (...) Breakthroughs come when people learn how to take the time to stop and examine their assumptions.'

PETER SENGE, OTTO SCHARMER ET AL. (88)

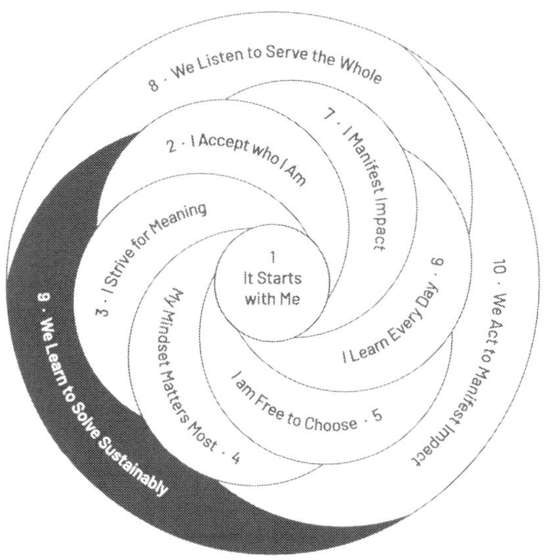

Have you experienced yourself, your team or your company running into the same problems or complex challenges repeatedly – feeling stuck regardless of all your attempts to find a solution? When feeling stuck, you are likely relying on solutions from the past – old ways of solving the problem – whereas complex challenges often call for a new way of seeing, sensing, thinking and solving. What got you here will not get you there. A jump in consciousness is required.

A jump in consciousness is like taking an elevator at the Eiffel Tower or any outdoor elevator of your liking. You look into other buildings on the ground floor and you have a perfect view of the city from the top floor. You travel effortlessly to have a bigger, broader and different view.

We can learn to travel much in the same way in our minds individually and collectively as an organization and, as we embrace a bigger and broader view, we can solve our problems in a new way. In fact, when we Listen Deeply, we often learn that the problem we thought was the problem wasn't the real challenge after all. Seeing our challenge from the top of the building or on a balcony often helps us realize this.

In Step Nine you will step out of your individual and collective assumptions - conscious or unconscious - to gain a new perspective, learning to solve sustainably. This means you do not only solve the right problem - equally important you solve it right at the root cause level. This means you do not waste several quick fix attempts including the cost, time, effort and energy tied into making quick fixes - jumping too fast into non-sustaining solutions.

Through practice it will become increasingly effortless for you to take the mind elevator with your colleagues every time it is needed. Your mind is your greatest asset or liability dependent on how you use it when it comes to achieving the output you want. I invite you to let go of fear of heights and instead choose to enjoy the view from up high through loving eyes.

Mindset mobility in action

You might object: 'But why should we change? We are doing well as the market leader.'

As businesses we risk becoming obsolete if we do not continuously adapt and evolve. Without a collective mindset that continuously stays in tune with our external conditions and expectations, we risk falling into complacency thinking - doing what we know best.

Organizations are not always as aware of the complacency trap. Do we take all the learnings from what Kodak, Blockbuster, Nokia and many other companies have experienced? These cases tell stories about companies not paying enough attention to what was going on in the market, not listening to their customers and not learning from their people.

Twenty-four-year-old engineer Steven Sasson from Brooklyn invented the process that allows us to take photos with phones, send images around the world in seconds and share them with millions of people. In 1975 Sasson created the first digital camera. It weighed 3.5 kg and the recording process took 23 seconds [89].

He proudly showed his invention to his boss, then to his boss's boss and, lastly, to the top team of the company he worked for. It was a prototype and the quality was not yet fantastic. Management were not impressed. They were convinced that no one would want to look at their pictures on a television set. 'Print has been with us for 100's of years and no one is complaining about inexpensive prints', was their response. They were afraid of cannibalizing their traditional business of films and physical pictures.

Sasson saw the emerging future and argued with the executives that you would not be able to sell film for long, but they would not listen to him. Sasson's technology disrupted the industry. Three years later, Kodak filed for bankruptcy. President Obama awarded Sasson the National Medal of Technology and Innovation in 2009 [90].

Kodak, Blockbuster and Nokia choose to protect and defend their current business with a mindset of 'playing not to lose'. It is easy to point fingers at them and companies alike. But could that not have happened to us, as well? Of course it could!

In our new and complex world of exponential change, we see other approaches taken by companies requiring experimentation, collaboration and people with deep-listening skills, including Google and Spotify.

Again and again we see challenges of one company becoming opportunities for other companies. The big question is how we turn our own challenges into opportunities without companies ceasing to exist.

Amazon is probably the single best example of a company constantly reinventing itself and its business models. It is relentlessly thinking differently, building new businesses next to the old ones, both complementary and cannibalizing.

For Amazon, protecting existing earnings is not a priority. The company is not afraid of challenging and losing existing business to build new and better. It is eager to grow and flourish. It is playing to win. From its start as an online bookstore, Amazon is now one of the leading providers of web services, a business quite far from the original retail core [(91)].

The same idea can work for you, your colleagues and your company; however, it requires that you suspend your own judgment ('I know best'), letting go of your cynicism ('We have tried this before') - and dance with your fear ('Will I and we be good enough?').

You might say, 'Yes, but then it is up to management to change as they often stand in the way of progress.'

You are right. It probably happens more often than we think. But isn't that just an excuse for not moving? What if we instead think not of hierarchies but of the organization as a living, breathing organism? Let's get inspired from our magical body.

You get a paper cut on your finger. First it hurts, and then what happens? As germs from the paper prepare to invade your body, your body springs into action. Your alarm system (platelets cells) alerts your immune system, your first line of defense (cytokines cells) rush to the scene and create swelling. Several of your cleaner-cells are waiting to manage the gems. Your jack-of-all-trades cleaners (neutrophils white blood cells) eat what does not belong.

If the problem is of more significant impact, you need the big eaters (the macrophages) that collect all kinds of garbage. The body automatically matches the invaders with different fighter cells in the body, so the response is balanced; not too little, not too much. When all the germs are eliminated and the body goes back to normal, it changes some of the cells which fought the infection into memory cells to remember the infection so they are well prepared for next time [92].

All that happens in a network of competent cells without a commander involved. Every cell knows its role trusting others to equally do their part, while getting smarter as they work on the problem. Indeed, this is something to be inspired by in a fast-paced world.

Back to us in business. When we are faced with complexity, we easily become overwhelmed and, from a mindset of fear, we are prone to creating either/or situations - seeking polarities, especially in times of change, complexity, resistance and pace. We seek polarities to establish simplicity in a complex world and to feel safe. As soon as you find yourself far into one polarity, you will create the other polarity.

The key is to listen to multiple stakeholders for you to better balance the needs of different stakeholders while being aware of your own polarity tendency. This is a lesson I learned myself by seeking the polarity of transformation. I would listen more to the voices of transformation rather than balancing with the critical voices calling out the need for driving performance [93].

Not helpful! Often, companies are not achieving this balance well, especially between the short-term performance and the long-term transformation. When we are not performing, many of us become fearful and move into survival mode and retreat into what feels like a safe and known space of a 'profit only' focus. Polarities and lack of balance are seldom good for business, at least not in the mid- to long-term.

How is your company balancing polarities? And how about you?

Pulled by partnership

Industry disruptions and the need for transformations can be initiated from many different sources, such as a change in customer needs, regulations, technology, demography, climate and health. One of the first transformations I actively participated in was for a very successful software company that had grown to more than 30,000 people in 30 years.

The company had become the de facto standard in the market, a true market leader. This meant for many years that customers were proactively calling our company, wanting our products, and our sales engine worked like a well-functioning machine, obtaining a significant market share.

Or so we thought! As we measured number of customers and total revenue, not level of engagement with clients, it took us a while to realize that although most companies were clients of ours, they only spent less than five percent of their total IT budget with us. We had a foot in the door, yet we were not fully inside and, therefore, not a strategic partner.

The day came eventually when our customers were no longer satisfied with being sold functions and features. Our sales force was 'aggressively waiting' for the telephone to ring, which was no longer happening.

Life became tough for the company and our salespeople started complaining. Daniel, who had been one of the best salespeople, complained the most: 'If only our customers would listen to us. We have what they need' he grumbled, and other salespeople joined him in arguing. A collective 'If only ...' culture was being developed and no one really moved (Step One).

I had recently joined as the HR director when Lucas, my visionary leader and CEO for the organization, came to my office with a draft of a new organizational structure. The organizational chart was not drawn as traditional boxes with reporting lines, but as a process overview of the value creation of our organization.

To the left on the paper our customers were illustrated with the rest of our organization lined up behind the customers in accordance with how we were working together to engage with and deliver solutions for our customers. Management was shown at the end of this process flow, to the far-right side of the paper. A very different view of the world, a different perspective than the usual hierarchies not showing the value creation of the company.

'Wow', I said, 'It is a tilted hierarchy!'. 'Exactly, Lucas smiled back, 'I want us to never forget why we are here! Wherever we are in the organization we serve our customers. We need to know our place and how we bring value to our customers. We are all in sales!'

We were both excited. I could already see how we needed to change our ways of working in HR to better serve our salespeople in serving our customers and the same was true for all parts of the organization. This started our journey putting customers in front of all of us.

Next time Daniel and the team were arguing, yearning for the past – 'If only our customers would listen' – Lucas passionately replied: 'Only if we listen to our customers, will we understand what they need and what we need to solve to serve them'.

As we started listening carefully to our customers, we understood that they did not want what we were trying to sell them. They did not want a simple product in one part of the organization but a fully integrated well-functioning solution that helped them to run better end-to-end as a company.

They wanted standardized, optimized value chains running seamlessly through their company as a whole and between companies enabled by the software we provided. They also wanted our software to openly and seamlessly integrate with other software products and solutions. They were looking for a partner to solve their problems, not a sales pitch.

We only had few people, if any, in our organization who could have these problem-solving conversations with our customers, let alone design solutions that would help our customers, knowing what was possible or not.

For us to truly partner up with our customers we needed to partner up in a different way with capabilities outside our company, partnering with consulting companies who had capabilities within business and process optimization as well as design of solutions. Capabilities that were needed to serve our customers properly.

The journey for our own people became significant. Initially they were frightened by the additional external sales and solution force, feeling they were losing out and losing control. They felt that something was being taken away from them. Hesitatingly at first, our salespeople went on sales training that included deep listening skills, a prerequisite for building solutions relevant for the customers. A big shift was needed. Daniel had been the best talker. Now, he needed to learn to become the best listener. He confessed he was scared about whether he would succeed.

He and his colleagues leaned into learning how to listen with care and curiosity, and they grew significantly through their new more facilitating role. They learned to inspire big multi-faceted engagement teams, now managing sales cases that often were more than 10 times bigger than before - at the same time creating much more value for our customers.

A win-win-win had been established. Our partners were happy, and it became a good business for us too, through training, to certify them in our software. We had moved from being a small IT provider into becoming a strategic partner for our customers, an eco-system and community builder.

What had been a critical challenge in our company's history turned into a huge opportunity. We dared to look at the world from a different view, not being constrained by the boundaries of our own company, instead thinking beyond entities. We were pulled by partnerships and a new operating model was established. We gained a new perspective: It is not what we can do on our own, but what we can create together that matters.

Now, it might sound rosy. It was a happy ending but, meanwhile, it became a serious change story for many people. We had to unlearn so many old habits – like me letting go of my pet projects in HR when they were not directly serving our customers. Our salespeople letting go of having full control of the access to our customers, trusting others to engage with what they saw as their customers. Moreover letting go of the belief that they had to know it all and instead create value by bringing the right team that together would bring and develop the needed knowledge.

We invited people to choose whether the way forward was something for them. Some people chose to leave, and others did not manage to make the shift and had to leave; the majority grew and moved to the new world.

Today, I continue to celebrate Daniel and his sales colleagues who had the courage to let go of their old ways of doing things. Despite their instant fear, they listened to the need of the customers and many of them adapted and evolved their mindset, leading to a very different level of solution selling benefitting all. They became the best sales organization I have ever met, focused on the customers' known and also unknown needs, passionately and constantly working on solving those needs. Today the company has grown to almost 100,000 people.

Lucas started the process by pausing, challenging our assumptions on what an organization looks like and how it serves in siloed functions, and allowing space for a new perspective to emerge. We teed up a collective mindset shift for all of us, moving from a mindset of optimizing our functions – for instance, me in HR – to finding out how we could generate value for our customers together, mentally all being in sales.

We changed from a mindset of 'We have to do it all ourselves to win' – a mindset of scarcity and protection – to 'We work with our partners to create win-win-win for all' – a mindset of openness and abundance. Our problems that kept us awake at night were created by us from a mindset of limitation, a burning platform representing the fear of how we could continue to make revenue.

We could, however, only solve our problems by moving towards a mindset of opportunity, a burning desire to serve our customers. We saw that shift in mindset - from Me to We - inspiring Lucas and all of us to see the opportunity in partnering with others. We saw there is more value creation for all parties involved - customers, colleagues, company and partners.

From this experience I learned how you can turn challenges into opportunities by having a different perspective on your business. This was huge for me - for the first time to see what I thought was a big problem turn into a huge opportunity. This is an experience and perspective I always carry with me in life.

When you have a different lens and hold a different mindset, you can make a different business - for example, by becoming an ecosystem and community builder, instead of an isolated company. Challenges that keep us awake at night are rarely solved sustainably alone but through partnering we find the right solution for the real problem.

What elements in this experience do you identify with in yourself or in your company?

Law, logic and love

You might ask: 'What is good place for me to start?'

In your decisions, I would say. We all make hundreds of decisions every day, which not only impact us but all those people around us - from our families, friends and colleagues to complete strangers. The decisions we make, and actions we take, matter. When we face a dilemma or an ambiguous and uncertain situation it is difficult to predict outcomes of our decisions using linear thinking. It is often not a straightforward Yes or No choice, but rather a more complex one.

You gain a better view and perspective of your decisions, allowing you to take sustainable long-term decisions by considering and balancing three dimensions: law, logic and love. These multiple perspectives activate your loving mindset. This goes for small and big decisions, in your personal and professional life.

1. **Law:** obedience or compliances with the law, policies and rules of the company.
2. **Logic:** reason, logic, intuition.
3. **Love:** care, love and compassion for all stakeholders impacted by the decision.

Which dimension do you think is most active for most of us at work?

Research conducted with more than 130,000 people across the globe shows consistently that the culture in many workplaces tends to increase the robotic compliance with rules, while we suppress care and empathy. Our consideration for the care of others impacted by our decisions is higher and often much higher in our personal lives than in our professional lives. We simply forget to bring our heart to work with us when we arrive in the morning (94).

Pause, connect and reflect. How does this step - We Learn to Solve Sustainably - make you think and feel?

In which situations would you typically be the person saying 'Let me fix this quickly, I want to win!' and in which situations are you the person saying 'Let's pause', 'What is needed now?', 'What opportunity is this challenge showing to us?' and 'What do we need to let go of to get there?'

Signature Practice: Step onto the Balcony

It is time to bring out your transformation journal, activating your heart and hands.

Why Step onto the Balcony?

Do you know the feeling of being so deeply involved in a task or a discussion that you lose sight of the bigger picture – being deeply into 'the dance' of your work? Entering the balcony has many benefits:

- **Reframe.** Turn business challenges into possibilities by reframing them
- **Perspective.** Identify the right root cause problem to solve sustainably
- **Awareness.** Become aware of your assumptions
- **Mindset.** Move through a mindset of fear to one of love
- **Patterns.** Explore the patterns and dynamics at play, including your own
- **Meaning.** Reminds you to be guided by what is important to you

To Step onto the Balcony provides an opportunity to learn and experiment and, when needed, choose a different approach. We use the metaphor of a balcony as it evokes the difference from being in 'the dance' – in the action – and gaining a new perspective when we Step onto the Balcony.

How To Step onto the Balcony

'Let's have a Balcony moment.' You call out and invite people to join you on the Balcony when you sense the need to pause your daily actions and zoom out.

On the balcony you explore one or all of the following questions to gain a new perspective:

- What do we notice?
- What are we not seeing?
- What is needed now?
- What becomes possible when we change our mindset (fear versus love)?
- What do we need to let go of and let come?

To act from this new perspective, we need to step down from the balcony and return to being 'in the dance' – in the action – of our work. The magic happens when we flawlessly alternate between the balcony ***and*** the dance, fully embracing one word: and.

You invite people to Step onto the Balcony when you:

- **are stuck** in a problem or a meeting, with the urge to give up
- notice that you revert to **old patterns**, old ways of thinking, old excuses, doing what you – individually and collectively – have always done
- want to have a **reflective moment** or to activate your creativity

Pause, connect and reflect

After using Step onto the Balcony as a practice for a period, cement your learnings.

How does Step onto the Balcony eliminate waste and bring value to you, your colleagues, your work, your company?

Using the practice frequently helps you build your adding-a-different-perspective-muscle, understanding the patterns of where you and your colleagues get stuck.

Have fun with getting new perspectives through The Balcony practice.

We are catching the bad guys

'Another regulation hampering business opportunities at work', Adam, an advisor with the bank, groaned. Adam's boss had asked him to get the job done now. At the same time, his boss expected him to increase revenue with his customers. Adam felt ashamed to call the customers to ask them about documentation regarding who they were and what they did for a living. He felt he was wasting their time. 'The Know-Your-Customer (KYC) regulation assumes you do not know your customers, but I do', Adam complained.

He had been working with the same customers for more than 10 years. Boy, how he longed for the good old days and, quite honestly, he had been putting off this work for a while – but his boss wasn't tolerating it anymore. It was clear it was time to bite the bullet and get it done.

Lisa had only been an advisor in the bank for a year. She was very excited to work with customers every day. She had given the KYC regulation some thought. She was attracted to banking as she saw how it also gave an opportunity for her to help catch the bad guys who took really terrible actions, such as trafficking and terrorism, identifying them through their financial criminal activity.

She loved sharing her passion with her customers and explaining why this KYC regulation was so important and how she saw they could partner up also with society around this task, which made her proud. Her burning desire to contribute to a greater good inspired the customers, who found her enthusiasm convincing. They too wanted to contribute to a better and safer society.

She explained the reason for the regulation was that we, in the past, as the financial sector and as a society, had not done a good job in stopping these criminals. Lisa explained to the customers that the bank was working on how to make the KYC filing easier for the customers, through digitalized solutions in the future, but until then, she hoped they would be willing to cooperate despite bumpy processes. As her customers understood the purpose behind the KYC activities, they accepted and appreciated the shared pain, which also built a stronger platform for relationships between Lisa and her customers.

Can you feel the difference between how Adam experienced the KYC regulation, compared to Lisa?

Adam saw it as a chore, another task he had to do to survive in his role. Lisa focused on what became possible and how to turn what could have been a challenge into an opportunity. She connected with her purpose and meaning in the work and that enabled her to view the situation through a different perspective. Yes, she took a balcony view.

She did not spend any negative energy on complaining about the regulations. Instead, she managed to grow the business with her customers, as well as managing what was required from the regulations. Fulfilling duty by finding her joy, she demonstrated a powerful combination and a recipe for success: matching what you love doing with how you contribute to other people and your company (Step Three).

Watching the impact, she made several of her colleagues adopt her approach. She became a positive force for the change she wanted to see in the world and her customers and colleagues followed her.

From Adam's and Lisa's experience we see how a difference in perspective can significantly influence your enjoyment at work and the impact you manifest when given exactly the same context, the same change: implementation of a new KYC regulation. Your individual as well as collective mindset determines whether you are able to turn a challenge into an opportunity.

From Adam's and Lisa's experience, what do you recognize in yourself and other people?

What got us here will not get us there

Transformation requires that we get a wider perspective. It requires a more integrated perspective and approach. What got us here will not get us there. We have to let go of old mindsets and invite new in.

The biggest letting go we possibly can make is letting go of the mindset of me-myself-mine, embracing we-ourselves-ours and moving from a space of ego to eco, requiring us to move from the field of fear to the land of love.

When we as company are under pressure and in fear, which is often the case during transformations, we default to focus on the familiar, the tangible and hard elements such as strategy, structure, processes, policies. We underestimate or wait with what is unfamiliar, soft, intangible, not easy observable - the human dimensions.

We need to measure the fear and waste of our human capacity - to make human potential quantifiable and tangible. The framework of Richard Barrett - inspired by Abraham Maslow's Hierarchy of Needs - allows us to measure the level of consciousness for individuals, organizations and communities. We get to understand the waste and value we create. We measure if we are making it - or breaking it [(10)(95)].

The most carefully strategized and thoroughly planned transformations are often blocked by our existing company culture pulling in another direction, 'eating the strategy' and vision. I have never seen business transformation succeed without a human transformation. They co-exist, co-thrive and co-evolve.

When we do not transform, our companies will not transform. It takes courage to lean into curiosity, leveraging a loving mindset to move mountains - and that we solve together as one, have everything we need to turn today's challenges into tomorrow's opportunities. And if we don't - our competitors will. Do you know that to be true?

Always, if you are in doubt or want to accelerate your transformation, say to yourself what you know to be true: *For any problem, we hold the keys to the solution.*

Before we move to the next step, note down your answer to the following question in your transformation journal.

As we solve our challenges, what do I need to let go of?

Step Ten: We Act to Manifest Impact

'And I continue to believe, that while no single conversation is guaranteed to change the trajectory of a career, a company, a relationship, or a life, any single conversation absolutely can.'

SUSAN SCOTT [96]

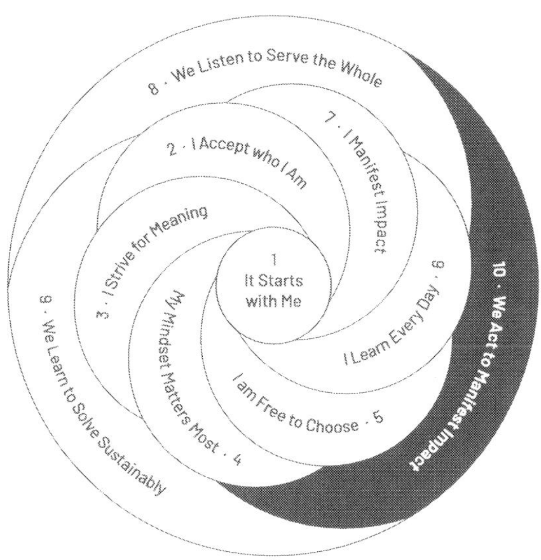

Individuals and institutions often lose their transformational momentum and return to where they started, slipping into old culture and behaviors. When we are stuck, we tend to we go back rather than breaking through the obstacles to achieve and manifest the impact we have travelled so far for. This has the risk of wasting the path we have walked so far, creating cynicism in the organization. I have experienced this waste of focus, effort, time, energy, agility and execution power when insight is not turned into actions and from there into impact.

Why?

Often, as companies, we have not managed to mobilize the full organization around the transformation, instead only relying on a devoted few in the executive team or in a transformation office.

It takes courage, stamina, persistency and patience to continue the journey, especially when people challenge it or when the going gets tough. When it is bumpy and blurry, courage is what will keep you on track, activating your individual and collective Player, also helping also other people to stay on track (Step Four).

Courage is the most important capacity to build in the School of Transformation. It is required in order to practice all Ten Steps of Transformation. Courage and transformation are co-travelers, best friends. Senior leaders all over the world are looking for leaders and people with courage, as they know that courageous people make transformation happen and stick [(97)].

If you don't feel you have much courage yet, don't worry: courage is a behavior, a capacity you can build. The more you practice courage, the better you become, the easier it becomes and the more confident you become. With your newly-gained confidence, you will step even further into courage until acting with courage becomes a healthy habit for you.

It is simple, yet not easy, as courage requires you to dance with your fear, including looking fear straight in the eyes when all your instincts tell you not to. It takes courage to choose a mindset of love step-after-step, especially if you are more familiar with a mindset of fear.

Your heart, the place for wise risks

You might challenge me: 'But that means I have to run a risk?'

Yes, indeed! Step Ten asks you to step into action together with your colleagues to follow through on the insights you have gained, the choices you have made and the actions you have already taken during the last Nine Steps. Step Ten builds on Step Seven: I Manifest Impact, igniting you to build healthy habits that sustain your transformation and keep you progressing until you reach the point of no return where you have made the breakthrough into a new way of being. The aim is to make the way of being and doing practiced second nature for you.

Step Ten calls for courage to stay true to what you now know to be true: courage to do what you know needs to be done, courage to do what is right, courage to go against the tide and challenge 'as is', courage to stay the course, courage to speak your truth to power. Courage is to welcome your fear as an indicator of your new opportunity for growth. Courage takes you further on the journey.

The English word 'courage' is derived from the Old French word '*Corage*', which means heart. Courage enables you to take wise risks with your heart. Courage requires that you are not in rigid control or denial of your fear, but rather that you calibrate the situation and accept your fear as part of human nature. You go through your fear to allow your heart to guide your behavior towards a worthwhile goal.

Qualities of courage include bravery, willingness to confront agony and tolerate pain, accepting uncertainty, the preparedness to do the right things, perseverance and patience. Without an appropriate balance between fear and confidence when facing a threat, you do not have the courage to overcome it [(98)].

You started with listening deeply to gain insight (Step Eight), you learned to solve sustainably and to make conscious choices (Step Nine) and now you want to take the needed actions and together manifest the desired impact for you, your team and your company (Step Ten).

Many people and leaders regret what they did not do when they had the chance; they had the insight but lacked the courage to make the change. We have seen the consequences of not daring in the cases of Kodak, Blockbuster and Nokia.

Consider all the times you know something is wrong and suspect other people do too, but don't speak up. Even in troubled companies, we passively resist new initiatives, observe struggles without helping and withhold resources. We hedge bets, hoard information, or go passive, which reinforces the decline of a company. It is so easy to choose fear before love, to choose caution before courage, both individually and collectively.

How is it in your company right now? Is more courage needed? Is your courage needed more?

If you don't speak up, you might never get there

In 1977, a KLM Boing 747 was getting ready to take off from the runway of the Canary Islands. On the flight was a 42-year-old highly experienced and top-notch first officer, as well as a 48-year-old flight engineer, flying together with one of the company's most senior pilots, their captain and chief flight trainer of the company's 747 pilots. A few months before, he had been the person testing and approving the first officer's ability to fly the 747 planes.

As the KLM flight lined up on the runway, the captain was impatient to take off and started moving the aircraft forward. The first officer implied that clearance had not yet been given but the captain did not pay attention to his comment. The first officer radioed the control tower and started the flight clearance reading when the captain suddenly interrupted with, 'We are going'.

At the same time another plane started to move along the runway. The control tower instructed the other plane to continue. The KLM flight engineer heard this and expressed his concern to the captain; however, the plane kept moving. At this point, neither the first officer nor the flight engineer said anything more. The conversation in the cockpit ceased and the KLM plane continued its take-off.

When all three of them finally saw the other plane blocking their way, it was too late [99].

Why did the first pilot and the flight engineer not continue to speak their truth? Even when putting your own life and other people's lives at risk, it can still be difficult to speak up with courage.

They had the choice (Step Five) to speak up. Their fear of authority, of being wrong, of being told off by their superior might have held them back. They knew there was a risk of them colliding with another plane, but they were not fully certain that it would happen. Even when the benefit of avoiding a possible collision was substantial, the benefits were delayed and not fully clear, while the cost – the fear of being told off by a superior – was immediate and very tangible. 583 people died that day. 583 lives were wasted. A tough example to share and even if we are not pilots, it is still relevant for all of us to reflect on.

How often do you make these trade-offs in important moments, choosing the immediate and tangible benefits?

If the first officer and flight engineer had Pressed Pause and chosen to act from a loving mindset – they would not have chosen to be silent. As informal or formal leaders, our role is to create psychological safety for people to be able to speak their truth. If we don't do that, we are losing out on so many voices that can help us progress and make the right choices. The investigation outlined the authority dimensions as one explanation for the crash [100].

It is for every one of us to help each other not to take fearful or fatal actions. We have no reason to believe that the captain had bad intentions when he said, 'We are going'. For some reason, he did not follow procedures, not paying attention or listening to what was being said to him. In that context, courage from the first pilot or the flight engineer was the only thing that could have stopped the planes from crashing.

It made me very reflective and sad to read this story. How many times have I not been acting like the captain without knowing? I can hear myself say: 'We are going' in other – thankfully less vital – situations and my team staying quiet.

How much waste have we created for ourselves and our companies? Me by not always creating the conditions for speaking up and people not always stepping up and doing what is right and needed regardless. As a leader, I deeply celebrate people daring to run the risk of also helping a 'captain stay on track', which does not in any way take away the responsibility of a leader.

Where do you on a daily basis speak your truth – or not? How are you supporting – or not – other people to speak their truth?

Being in the arena

You might say: 'Not a lot of courage is needed in my job. After all, I'm not a pilot.'

Courage is what is needed for you to show up in the arena. If you are not in the arena, you are not in the game. That makes you an observer, a Tourist. Step Nine helped you learn to alternate from the balcony to the dance and back again. This is an important capacity to build on in Step Ten, enabling you to sense: What is needed now?

Through courageous conversations you work with and build on the healthy tensions present in your company, integrating and balancing different dimensions of the transformation. By inviting for multiple perspectives on a matter to foster better solutions and decisions, you keep progressing as a team and as a company.

The powerful balance comes when you progress executing on your plans with conviction and yet are willing to go back and take a new path as you gain new insight. As we learned in the KLM story, stepping into courage might not feel safe, but it will keep us safe.

In a study where 200 CEOs were followed for one decade, they concluded that courage is the one characteristic that defines the greatest talents over time. Courage is needed for accepting yourself, constantly adjusting, evolving and renewing yourself and impacting your surroundings to do the same. It takes courage to face this realization head-on and act on it without hesitation or drama, staying resourceful, relevant and resilient [97].

Pulled by potential

In 2011, a giant company I had the joy to work for had been reduced from 430,000 to 115,000 people. The share price was dangerously low, and a hostile takeover was becoming a real option. We were at risk of joining the large and growing club of companies that did not make it.

I had the privilege to join the company the day our new CEO, James, started. He immediately and courageously launched a 360-degree all-inclusive transformation, which included building a new business system and operating model for the company.

Forty-five days into his job, he hosted a leadership meeting with the top 100 leaders where he, in a 'balcony moment' presented a new view of the world based on the insight he had gained during four months of listening to hundreds of customers and investors and thousands of colleagues across the world. His interviews had also uncovered significant cultural waste such as unproductive behaviors of blame, shame, them versus us, lack of accountability, lack of innovation, conflict and risk avoidance, reflecting a largely fear-based culture.

The fact that James had gathered and shared with us the insight with such a high level of honesty and transparency made our situation overwhelmingly clear. I vividly remember the reflective and somber energy among our leaders sitting together for the first time listening to him.

This also became our first collective Courageous Conversation, addressing the major issues and tensions in the room. We acknowledged aspects of the company we had chosen not to see or act on, while it suffered more and more. It was tough yet energizing to get it out in the open!

I sensed how people started breathing again following the openness. We built a fact-based case for change and a compelling story of the potential our company had, and what was needed from each of us and together to realize that potential. That was the start of our transformation journey, which we positioned as a marathon not as a sprint, knowing that it would take years, requiring stamina, patience and resilience. The architecture of the transformational program catered for a 360-degree approach balancing: Why, How and What; minds and hearts; performance and transformation.

We focused on five priorities for the transformation:

1. Customer Centricity; aligning our organization around our customers.
2. Resource to Win; value creation from everybody, redistributing resources to win.
3. End to End; aligning people and processes along the value chain.
4. Operating Model; aligning the full organization to support priorities 1-3.
5. Performance and Growth Culture; building the mindset to deliver on priorities 1-4.

The five priorities remained the same throughout the whole journey. The Performance and Growth Culture became the foundation of the transformation permeating all priorities.

A corporate highway of service

With 82 businesses units and an endless amount of different business models it was nearly impossible to serve our customers with the needed speed, agility and quality. Technological innovation and entrepreneurship had been the reason for our company's enormous success in the past and hence product developing units operated as if they were the kings, deciding what to develop for our customers.

We needed to establish new ways of working which put the sales organization – who were now being told what to sell – and our customers – in the absolute center of our attention, creating a highway through the organization to serve our customers. Complementary multifunctional teams were put together along the value chain – the highway – to remove speed bumps and barriers for execution and to shift the power structure towards the customers and the people directly serving them.

Although having delivered to the same customer groups, many people had never met each other before connecting across their departments. As we included our customers in the work, we could for the first time accomplish a 360-degree perspective for our challenges, which over time led to much better solutions.

This work in the new teams started off being quite challenging for people as they were still holding on to their old units and mindsets. Through significant training and development of Transformational Capacity within the teams organized around the customers, we enabled mindset shifts in support of our customers and our journey.

Instead of being compliant and avoiding risk, we stimulated passion and commitment. Instead of seeking harmony and silo mentality, we stimulated collaboration, challenge and support. Instead of self-interest – me-myself-I – we stimulated a focus on a common good for the company. Instead of hiding and green washing, we stimulated transparency, honesty and courage to speak up.

We secured that each team had equal representation of performance -oriented and transformational competencies with influencing power and that everyone was invited to belong with an equal voice. We learned how to have Courageous Conversations, which was a prerequisite to moving from a harmony seeking culture in fear of 'breaking the relationsship'. And move to a culture where we could challenge 'as-is' and each other for the benefit of raising the bar, understanding that tension was healthy, maximizing the learning when we leveraged each other's complementary competencies and capacities.

To fuel transformation and performance simultaneously, we organized around granular units consisting of 400 business (product development) and market (sales) combinations with joined business objectives and a collaborative profit and loss. No one had ever heard about a collaborate P&L for 400 collaborative units/cells before, where success could only happen via clear ownership and collaboration between product development and sales.

The full transparency around each business-market-combination allowed us to constantly raise the bar supported by the principle 'Green helps Red become Green'. This meant when you were the best, you shared with the rest. Collectively we moved our mindset from Me to We, supported by clear principles and processes. Business reviews shifted from spending 70 percent of the time looking backward into financials, to spending 70 percent on forward looking elements – the enablers and solutions for success.

'Are there any Courageous Conversations you need to have, that you have not yet had?' was often the question asked by senior leaders to the teams, encouraging the conversations to take place within the teams without senior leaders interfering. As we embedded it into our review processes, having Courageous Conversations started becoming a new norm. Although difficult at first, they moved into becoming a habit. This is how we do it around here, this is our culture. If you want to belong, you build your capacity to have Courageous Conversations as this is important for our business. As we practiced, fear of having a Courageous Conversation significantly reduced.

Afterwards, leaders who had been part of the transformation pointed to having the discipline around Courageous Conversations as one of, if not the, most important element for succeeding with the overall transformation.

Focus, impact and joy

Despite general excitement and strong momentum around our journey, the steam faded two years into the journey, as people were exhausted from the size and duration of the transformation. It felt like having two jobs - one of performance and one of transformation. This was concerning as we were not halfway through the marathon and there were many sprints yet to come. In fact, we needed to increase and sustain our pace.

We realized that sustained performance does not work without organizational health. If we had paid earlier attention to the health of the organization, we most likely would have been able to reduce the exhaustion people felt, leading to a deteriorating engagement also among our leaders.

We realized that time is a finite resource and we ran out of hours. Instead we needed to support all of us to expand our energy, our infinite resource. We stimulated people to holistically take care of their health - body, emotions, mind and spirit - granting them to sustain peak performance over time. We strove to find the right balance between constantly raising the performance bar while securing development and recovery for everyone. We became much better at prioritizing and focusing on what really mattered and brought value, having the courage to say 'No' to elements bringing less value. Having the courage to take our health seriously.

To drive the dialogue on health consistently throughout the organization we added one impactful question in the quarterly performance check-in between people leaders and their people: 'How do you enjoy?' This question was added in addition to the already existing questions, including: 'How do you perform?', and 'How do you develop?'. The 'How do you enjoy?' question facilitated dialogues around whether people were in flow and balance with their work, whether they did what they liked to do most and found the meaning in their work (Steps Three, Six and Seven). It was simple and powerful!

This holistic approach to organizational health allowed us to find ways to work smarter not harder. As the energy expanded for every one of us, engagement returned, output and performance kept increasing. Together, as a company, we acted and manifested impact.

Culture, a real enabler

During this transformation an incredible dormant capacity and potential in our organization was released. Everybody was invited to shift their mindset as a critical part of our culture transformation. Invited to step into their own potential to innovate and partner with a new level of agility and commitment with a shared passion to create value for our customers. Leveraging healthy tensions, having Courageous Conversations, failing fast and asking for help became the critical Transformational Capacity we built.

Our CEO, James, along with many people in the organization, had an incredible ability to leverage all our culture practices in many of the actions he took or facilitated. In this way he helped maintain our new level of consciousness and practices, being extremely robust and consistent also when the transformation during periods was bumpy and blurry. Consistently, we leveraged our new capacity to find solutions and break through one challenging situation after the other, staying the course, together.

We mobilized the majority of the organization by activating and involving the units with simple, timely and relevant messages. With our programs we reached and connected with well-educated headquarter people, as well as passionate and devoted factory workers. This was a brave move. Without the leaders' strong conviction of people's potential and the willingness to invest, we might have missed this key success factor.

James was pulled by the potential he saw in this company and he knew that time was running out as we were losing our relevance. Many people expressed how they moved from fear and fatigue, realizing that this was a once in a lifetime opportunity where they could release their own, and their company's, full potential.

From this experience I learned how important it is to integrate and balance human and business transformation into everyday business. To build Transformational Capacity in everyone – every day on the job, trying and testing until thriving. Nothing beats impact made together.

What elements in my experience do you identify with in yourself or other people?

In a study, 1,000 leaders were asked to list behaviors their team members had which earnt their trust. The most common answer was asking for help. Leaders were not inclined to delegate important work to people who did not habitually ask for help as the leaders did not trust that they would raise their hands when they needed help. Asking for help requires courage.

This comes more easily for some people than for others. Studies show that your perception of your standing in an organization can affect your level of courage. Employees are more likely to act courageously when they have social power advantages over other people. This means that the further down in the organization we are, the harder it is to step into courage. A concrete way to lower the barriers is to step into courage and have courageous conversations as a healthy habit. Most companies I have worked for have implemented this consistently to benefit everyone and the company [(101)].

Pause, connect and reflect. How does this step – We Act to Manifest Impact – make you think and feel?

Is your habit saying: 'Someone else is probably going to speak up?' Or are you typically more the person saying: 'What is needed now?', 'What is the right thing to do for the totality?'

Signature Practice: Have Courageous Conversations

It is time to bring out your transformation journal, activating your heart and hands.

Why Have Courageous Conversations?

You might be shying away from addressing tension you have with someone that you feel prevents you from progressing in your work, draining your energy and taking up space in your mind. You might be telling yourself it is not that important and perhaps you do not feel safe to address what you have noticed. Conflicts arise when you do not communicate how you feel and what your needs are.

Having Courageous Conversations helps you to achieve all of the following:

- **Tension release.** Address your tension that can release your burden and free up energy. Tension is a massive waste collector.
- **Healthy tension.** Welcome tensions, many of which are healthy; when addressed openly and with curiosity they help you progress.
- **Opportunities.** Step into courage, take ownership for your part of the tension, invite co-creation of new opportunities, solutions and shared learning.
- **Relationships.** Build trust through honesty, releasing wasted energy – trapped in fear and frustration – for productive work. Take your relationships to a new level.
- **Break down barriers.** Break down barriers for execution, to progress faster with more impact.
- **Transformation.** Breakthrough in your and other people's transformation when done with compassion and courage.

By transforming relationships, you transform businesses, allowing you and them to continue to flow, flourish and function.

How to Have Courageous Conversations?

Preparation
Think about a person you want to have a Courageous Conversation with because of the waste created by not having it (Waste in terms of energy, focus, progress, mistakes, important things not said and done, impact).

A Courageous Conversation is a heart-to-heart conversation where your level of self-awareness and preparation is vital.

Phase 1: Press Pause (Step Five)

What is going on for you?

- What is your trigger (tension)?
- What needs of yours are not being met?
- What might be going on for the other person?

Phase 2: Make a Choice

Be clear about the situation

- What is your part in it? (taking ownership for your part)
- What are you curious to understand?

Phase 3: Set a positive intention

- What would you like the conversation to create for both of you (connection, growth, learning ...)?
- How will you show up to enable this?

Phase 4: Have the Courageous Conversation

1. In one sentence, I want to talk about ... [the tension] and it is my intention to ... [your intention].
2. When I observed ... [factual observations, non-judgmental], I felt ... [your feeling] because I have a need for ... [why it is important for you].
3. My part in this is ... [taking ownership for your part].
4. I am curious about how you felt and what your needs are? ... [listen deeply].
5. What do we want to co-create? [both co-creating next steps]

If it feels like too much to remember, don't worry! The most important is your intention. It does not matter if you manage the process to perfection; your conversation partner will connect and respond to your intention, sensing if you mean well for you both.

Don't have a conversation if you are still dressed up with the handcuffs of a Prisoner or the sun hat of a Tourist, wanting to make the other person wrong. Courageous Conversations are for Players (Step Four).

Courageous Conversations are important business

- Have **compassion** for yourself.
- Start **small** before big conversations to gain confidence with someone you trust.
- Set a **positive intention** and listen deeply, be curious and ask questions.
- Allow **silence** to do the heavy lifting of the process.

Make a list for yourself of all the Courageous Conversations you have not had that you would have benefitted from having. Consider if some of them are still relevant to have.

Find yourself a Courageous Conversation Buddy who you can share your commitments and learnings with, someone potentially on a similar transformation journey as you.

Pause, connect and reflect

After using the Have Courageous Conversations practice for a period, cement your learnings.

- How is it for you to have these talks? What do you celebrate? What do you learn?
- Do you manage to stand by your intentions and how do your conversation partners experience your talks?
- Do you manage to create a positive outcome for you both?
- What is the value created for your company when you and your colleagues have the Courageous Conversations you need to have?

It is much more important that you have Courageous Conversations than try to become perfect at doing it.

Do something courageously, every day. That alone will transform your life.

I am not my brain?

James had been a successful CEO for many years. His body carried his brain – at least that was how he thought for many years. He was convinced – and had proven – that his incredible IQ, analytical mind and intensity were his main forces until he realized, 'Oh, I have a heart as well'.

Incredibly smart as he was, he understood that he had not acknowledged the potential of his heart. He had made his career by focusing on the hard stuff and he was great at it. Yet, he understood that what took him here would not take him there; he needed to also understand how to lead the soft part of his company to get people to follow him. James always wanted the real deal; half-baked was not his cup of tea.

His courage helped him to immerse himself in a deep leadership program where he came to understand much more of his inner self – where he accessed his Emotional Intelligence as an add-on to his well-developed IQ [(28)]. The world opened up for him. He understood that not everything of importance can be measured and calculated or found in an Excel sheet, which was quite a revelation to him.

When he took on the role as CEO of a company that had a history of more than 130 years and employed more than 115,000 people, he developed into a whole leader, integrating his head, hands and heart. From this place, he could now courageously lead a deep transformation of the company balancing performance and health.

'Our culture can make or break our company!' James looked at me with conviction, as we detailed what elements were important to include in our culture transformation and how to make it an integral part of the overall business transformation. He passionately repeated this message at the first leadership summit with our top 100 leaders, where we launched the transformation.

I saw him inviting himself into one Courageous Conversation after the other. Leaning in, deeply listening and learning. He called out any tension he saw and helped the rest of us to do the same. Aiming to unlock the potential of the company, he was willing to run the risk of being criticized, of making mistakes. He showed us all how to put the overall purpose of the transformation ahead of our fear, in the pursuit of progress. The more we did this together, the better we became. Stepping into courage was something we could learn, like flexing any other muscle. When we realized this big potential, it was easier for us to get out of our own way.

Today, when James looks back at this transformation, he is convinced that culture was the real deal – the secret to success and a competitive force that allowed the company to get ahead of the game. This company's transformation is now recognized as one of the most successful transformations in the world. The essence of it was integrating the hard and soft in each step of the way, with a clear roadmap about how to transform and perform in synchronicity. It started with James's understanding that it had to start with him and his own journey.

He is a perfect example of what happens when you decide to be the change you want to see in the world. His personal journey included many, if not all, of the Ten Steps we have co-travelled in this book. It was not obvious for him from the start and it was not always easy for him to combine hard with soft and put equal focus on the Why, How and What.

The fact that he was struggling and that he was honest about it made him much more credible. The journey was worthwhile for him and the many other people he led throughout the transformation, constantly seeking to improve people's lives way beyond the people in the company and its customers.

From James's experience we learn that the success of the outer game, what is going on in the business transformation, is dependent on the quality of the inner game, what is going on inside every one of us. A well-functioning inner operating model is a condition for a well-functioning business operating model. As an integrated whole human being, leading with head, heart and hands, James successfully lead this truly effective and rewarding transformation.

Where do you recognize yourself or other people in this experience?

Balancing performance and transformation

Business transformations are full tensions. How can we see them as healthy and welcome them?

Many business transformations fade or fail, lacking the ability to balance transformation and performance or manage the healthy tension between the two - having the needed Courageous Conversations. We run for and chase the quarterly results to serve impatient shareholders.

When you add a transformation on top of your daily operations, you risk losing focus on your performance and many companies experience a dip in performance for a period during a transformation. This is a vulnerable phase for the transformation. We get scared; shareholders get impatient and activist owners might enter the scene, identifying a performance gap they want to benefit from.

The best we can do - to secure a transformation to make it to its breakthrough - is to put equal focus on performing and transforming. Not losing sight of performance is critical, however, guided by the transformational direction. Performance is the license to transformation!

Tackling the consequences when performance is slipping or when we ourselves, our colleagues or the transformation slide, slip, slow down or become stuck is critical for a successful path - a missing element for many companies. We put the company at risk when we don't have the stamina and patience to stay the course - instead wasting all the investment made. With a loving mindset, we do not choose for convenience, popularity and complacency. We do what is needed - as if it was our own company - acting with courage.

Always, if you are in doubt or want to accelerate your transformation, say to yourself what you know to be true: *I am a bold and brave transformer.*

Before we move to the next step, note down your answer to the following question in your transformation journal.

As you step into courage, what is needed now for the collective?

PART IV

It's Time To Act

From Insights to Impact

'Life is a challenge, meet it;
Life is an opportunity, seize it;
Life is a gift, discover it'

KAREN TOBIASEN

Thank you for allowing me to be your co-traveler in your transformational journey. You might already have a long history of transforming yourself and your businesses that you are building on. Here you have explored the beauty of love, danced with your fear and walked the Ten Steps of Transformation.

You may have found it easy, and you may at times have struggled. You may have put all the practices into play or selected a few to start with. No matter which path you have chosen for your journey, I imagine you sense the opportunity to disrupt and enrich your life through love and laughter.

Pause, connect and reflect

Before you move further into the last pages of this book, take a moment to pause, connect and reflect – as you have done so many times throughout this book and journey.

Have you given yourself the gift of those precious moments for yourself?

The book offers you tools to accelerate your transformation. How are you relating to them?

Are you explaining to yourself that you are inspired but you will try to implement them later – potentially dancing with your Tourist?

Are you arguing why these practices would not work for you and your surroundings – potentially engaging with your Prisoner?

Or are you in the middle of implementing the practices, including living with the ups and down accompanying any real implementation – activating your Player?

The best day to start was yesterday. The next best day is today!

Implementation tales of transformation

As I wish for you that this book leaves a lasting impact in your life, I want to provide you with more than just insights. There are three dimensions that are particularly helpful to sustain implementation:

Taking micro steps: Your brain is lazy. It shifts to autopilot, doing what you have always done as soon as you don't pay attention.

Tobias got excited every time a new book arrived. 'Hurrah!' he thought, always hoping that the next book would help him change. They never did. He kept repeating his pattern of gaining more insight, with limited impact. Recognizable?

Tobias's breakthrough came in a dialogue with a friend, who shared how he made micro steps every day towards better. His only commitment to himself was 10 minutes of absolute attention on the change he was working on implementing. Same time, every day – just before his lunch break. When the change had become second nature, he moved onto the next change.

When a change is too big, your brain is eager to give up or tell stories about why it can't happen. Your brain is flexible, especially with micro steps repeated every day. It will adapt when you take charge. This is the reason why I invite you to join The Heart Revolution community that can provide you with many more tools, exercises and practices to continue to assess, build and sustain your Transformational Capacity.

For more details, see the section 'Welcome to the Heart Revolution' at the end of the book.

The essence is: It works when you work it [(102)].

What change do you want to work on?

Best buddies: Did you manage to team up with a transformation buddy? How has that been for you and your process?

Silas and Sofie were working in the same team. Their leader was highly passionate about the team's personal growth and transformation and decided to implement the Signature Practices within the team. Silas and Sofie did not know each other that well at the beginning yet ended up becoming great transformation buddies.

As time was limited, they established a routine of talking on their way to work - Silas in his car and Sofie walking. Sofie was inspired by affirmation sentences like, *'I am the perfect CEO of my life'*, and enjoyed sharing her intentions and thoughts with Silas, who was a great listener.

Sofie supported Silas, who was more hesitant to work through his many explanations and excuses for why he should or could not do 'the work' by patiently and repeatedly asking him: 'Is that really true?' And often the stories Silas told himself were not true, leading to the real conversation about what was really going on for Silas.

They laughed together about their Prisoner and Tourist behaviors making their life and learning feel easier. It is probably the most profound buddy-pair I have ever witnessed. They cared, dared and shared.

With whom do you dare to share?

Celebrating Community: Some teams have taken the work even further. Every fortnight they meet for drinks or dinner, discussing the progress of their individual transformations. They agree on a challenge for the next 14 days - for example, having a Courageous Conversation that had been waiting or speaking their absolute truth in each Check-In, noticing the impact on themselves and their colleagues.

During the gathering they celebrate each other – the daring, caring, vulnerability and courage they show. They feel seen and celebrated by each other in their journey, especially when things are difficult, learning from each other. This accelerates their individual and collective transformation. The power of community is very visible. Together you travel much further. What transformation tribe are you part of?

Take this quiet moment to reflect upon the challenges, opportunities and gifts life offers you right now. I wish for you to disrupt; I wish for you to enrich. Life is precious and I wish this book to have been worthwhile reading for you!

We are our culture

Your business is dependent on you transforming. The culture in a company reflects the collective mindset of the individuals working in and with it. It is not separate from us. We are the culture. When you transform, it transforms. With the collective mindset we hold we can either make or break a company.

The Signature Practices drive behaviors – what we do and do not do – and thereby create culture. When we all know and use the same practices, we can challenge and support each other, allowing us to grow faster together, holding each other accountable while moving from a statement to a commitment to make a positive change.

The Signature Practices give our companies and colleagues a common language and a common way to build Transformational Capacity – individually as well as collectively. They facilitate a shift in our mindset and allow us to step into a mindset of love – for us to enjoy, grow and contribute at a higher impact level.

Higher impact is created through elimination of waste such as judging, blaming, avoiding, defending, protecting, delaying, politicizing, fighting, sub-optimizing, camouflaging and repeating failures, low engagement, energy, intensity and problem-solving capacity – to mention a few. Transforming company cultures means shifting mindsets at individual and collective level.

This is how we change a workplace from one of competing agendas and conflicts to one of alignment and balanced focus. We reduce bureaucracy and politics and increase the quality of execution by challenging the corrosive idea that work 'is just a job', instead embracing that workplaces are where we can unleash our potential and uplift our spirit (17).

I encourage you to take the lead to create environments that embrace a loving mindset to be tested, challenged, moved and adopted.

There is no business transformation without a human transformation

I have seen transformations fail or fade because we underestimated the human part of the transformation, focusing solely or predominately on what we thought we could measure – not fully integrating the culture transformation. As humans we tend to default to what is familiar when we have a challenge or dilemma – so too do companies.

When a company is under pressure, as it often is during a time of transformation, we default to solving challenges in ways we know from the past. We focus on the tangible and hard elements such as strategy, structure, processes and policies because we don't know how to address the intangible and softer parts such as our mindsets and culture. The most carefully strategized and thoroughly planned transformations with clear road maps can therefore be blocked by the existing culture of the organization pulling in another direction through people's resentment, resistance and rejection. In essence, this is waste created by you and me, costing companies and societies – and thereby you and me – money, focus, effort, time, energy, agility, execution power and eventually our capacity to solve and create impact.

The body cannot breathe without its capillaries, the tree cannot breathe without its leaves and a business cannot breathe without you and me being the change we want to see. We can only manifest impact when we are all fully mobilized, together turning challenges into opportunities as we listen, learn and act in a new way everywhere in the organization.

When we all embrace and learn from the Ten Steps of Transformation, we will enable our own human transformation, and thereby our business transformation. The enrichment of human beings enriches businesses and vice versa, resulting in more enriched lives in general. And as we spiral through this virtuous cycle, we will see beautiful ripples expanding into societies and beyond.

Are you ready to continue your transformation journey?

A Life of Meaning, Mindset & Manifestation

'You are the perfect CEO of your life'

KAREN TOBIASEN

I am privileged to always carry the story of Sarah and her short 32 years of life in my heart, reminding me that life is brief and precious, increasing my desire for you and me to live life to its fullest. As you have built your Transformational Capacity through the Ten Steps of Transformation you have actively worked with your meaning, mindset and manifestation.

Why: A matter of a greater meaning

What are you living for?

When I ask people this question I often hear similar answers, such as: 'I want to be happy and healthy', 'I want to make a positive difference' or 'I want to learn and develop'. All variations of balancing enjoying, growing and contributing privately as well as professionally.

Similar themes emerge when listening to the top five regrets from people in palliative care during the last 12 weeks of their lives [103]:

1. I wish I'd had the courage to live a life true to myself, not the life other people expected of me.
2. I wish I hadn't worked so hard.
3. I wish I'd had the courage to express my feelings.
4. I wish I had stayed in touch with my friends.
5. I wish that I had let myself be happier.

No one wanted more money, a fancy car, a bigger title or 22 castles. When we reflect on what really matters to us – either in friendly dialogues or on our deathbed – we return to the essence of who we are with a desire for a loving mindset and greater meaning. Those questions of meaning, purpose, love and well-being are what make us human beings. That is what our consciousness allows us to ponder on. When we do not ask ourselves these questions early or often enough, they might show up later in life as a life crisis – a feeling of meaninglessness – and a sense that work and life don't have enough to offer and that we are not fulfilled.

Mankind and the moon

Stephen Hawking writes: 'One of the great revelations of the space age has been the perspective it has given humanity on ourselves. When we see the Earth from space, we see ourselves as a whole. We see the unity, and not the divisions. It is such a simple image with a compelling message; one planet, one human race.'

Hawking is often referenced as a powerful example of someone who beat all the odds that were placed against him – becoming one of the most celebrated scientists and having a rich family life despite battling a severe case of ALS. And yet he too publicly shared that he had gone through significant periods of defeat and contemplation of giving up. Ultimately, however, he found meaning in life in trying to answer the big questions of the universe – passionate about finding a way forward for people of our world [(104)].

On July 20, 1969 humankind united to watch the first man walk on the moon. It brought us together in a meaningful moment. The 'man on the moon moment' was an antidote to the significant amount of fear present in the world at that time, including the assassination of the Kennedy brothers John F. and Bobby, the Cold War and the Vietnam War [(105)].

When we detect fear between each other, it would serve all of us well to revisit a picture of our planet from space every so often and ask ourselves how, instead of dividing with fear, we can unite in a common meaning of wanting a bright future for our planet, for our human race. Do you take time to ask yourself and people around you these questions? Are you rushing through life, not fully realizing that you have more potential to unfold?

Work has the potential to become your life enricher and a great place where you can realize your meaning. It is an invitation to all of us to find a role where we can live our passion - what we love doing - with the condition that it contributes to others and serves the overall purpose of the company.

When your passion and purpose align well with that of your company, you are in the best possible place. If not, it is time to consider a change. The big Why, the meaning and purpose of life, can sometimes be challenging to identify. For all of us. You might want to revisit Step Three.

What meaning are you welcoming into your life?

How: A matter of a loving mindset

'What are you looking for?'

I, along with many of my fellow Danes, was brought up with an existentialistic life perspective, including that life has no meaning in itself. Life has the meaning we give it. Life is neither fair nor unfair; it simply is. Meaning in our lives is created by each and every one of us.

This freedom to take responsibility for our lives can create anxiety and fear, as well as opportunities and autonomy. Every action we take can create fear or freedom. There is no one to blame. You own it. I own it. We are it. Choice, ownership, authenticity, integrity, freedom! I wonder if this philosophy and attitude to life is a significant reason for the Danes being some of the happiest people in the world? It activates the Players in all of us.

These existentialist beliefs are rooted in our Danish culture, thanks to our philosopher Soeren Kirkegaard, who is considered to be the world's first existentialist philosopher. At the core of his work, he brings us back to ownership for our life (Step One). He argues that each individual is responsible for giving meaning to their life and living it passionately, sincerely and authentically. While this might be a common thought in our time, it was not mainstream thinking in the late 1800s and early 1900s, although it quickly gained popularity. The biggest value of existentialism is freedom. The greatest virtues are authenticity and integrity in accepting who you are (Step Two) living with congruence and consistency.

We seek to define our existence apart from the labels we traditionally put on ourselves or other people – for example, doctor, father, mother, nurse, senior vice president. What we or other people 'should be, must be, or ought to be'. Instead we identify with our essence – who we are and how we operate without the labels. We genuinely acknowledge another person with 'I see you', equally feeling that they see us as the whole human being we are.

The responsibility you have as an individual can both be challenging and incredibly liberating. You are the master of your own experience. Your awareness of your context, conditions and situation allows you to take conscious choices, moment by moment. The mindset shift that holds the greatest potential for you, and for all of us, irrespective of which organization we work for and where we are in life, is the mindset shift from fear to love.

As you have seen, stepping into your Player mindset helps you turn your challenges into opportunities. As you step into a mindset of love rather than fear you contribute by co-creating your own and your company's future a little faster and further. A loving mindset enables you to see opportunities in challenges, to learn from upsets, to meet other people with curiosity and compassion, co-creating and manifesting impact together.

You might already have noticed a shift in your language. When you connect to yourself and hold a mindset of love, you are in the world of 'will, want, and can'. When you are driven more by external comparison, you are driven from fear; you are in the world of 'ought, must, and should'. Consider when you are swaying with your Prisoner or Tourist or fully activated in your Player.

Kirkegaard teaches that to venture is to lose the foothold momentarily, whereas not to dare is to lose oneself. Stepping into courage can make you lose your feeling of safety, belonging and self-worth for a while until you find yourself again, now in a new expanded version.

Courage helps you all the way. It helps you accept who you are (Step Two) and it helps you balance staying safe and comfortable with always seeking to expand. The work you do for yourself, bringing awareness (Steps One-Four), choice (Step Five) and practice (Steps Six-Seven) deliberately into your life will set you apart – being resourceful, relevant and resilient building your Transformational Capacity.

What mindset shifts are you welcoming into your life?

What: A matter of manifesting impact

What are you longing for?

My longing is that we together build the great workplaces we deserve to have. I imagine that when our grandchildren ask us, 'What were the best moments in your life?', we will answer: 'Well, I remember many beautiful moments with my family and friends and also one time I worked in an organization with a community of people who I will never forget, because together we ...'.

Letting go of 'mine' and 'yours'

Those memories are formed in environments of love – also at work! What does it mean to bring a loving mindset to work every day? What does it mean for business to live a loving mindset?

Kirkegaard did not talk about business, yet we gain inspiration from him on how to live love in a business context through his thoughts and work. How love can be translated into every day in a business. He described love – universal, not romantic love – as being a 'you' and an 'I', whereas there is no love in 'mine' and 'yours' because these are words which reflect possessions and separation. The more 'mine' and 'yours' disappears, the more we embrace a loving mindset. Love is the process of becoming 'one' letting go of 'mine' and 'yours', without losing 'you' and 'me'.

Fear desires words like 'mine' and 'yours'; fear wants possessions and protection. In a business setting, a feeling of possession, feeling entitled and attached, can lead to significant waste – for example, 'my people', 'my results', 'my budget', 'my idea' and 'my this and that'.

Even in companies that have been truly suffering, I have experienced people holding on to 'my'. For example, when we asked people to save money, some people responded with 'I am within my budget, so I can travel. The travel freeze must be for the rest of the company, not for me'. With that mindset, no wonder the company was suffering.

With a mindset of love, there is no 'my budget', but rather 'the company's budget', with the total performance and health of the company as everyone's focus. The word 'my' is a relevant word combined with 'my responsibility', 'my ownership', 'my contribution', 'my attitude', 'my mindset' and 'my results'.

We are used to being measured and also measuring ourselves through our results, which is important, as long as our individual results are not sacrificing the impact we manifest as a company together – as a unity. In the companies I have been part of we struggled with silo thinking while yearning to come together as one. To mobilize and unite as one force rather than separate. It is a constant struggle in business; are we optimizing for the parts or for the whole?

Moving from an 'I-me-mine' mindset towards a 'we-us-ours' mindset releases a significant amount of energy that is tied into defending and protecting our own turf. It is also a struggle between short-term gains and long-term rewards, expressed by the saying 'If you want to go fast, go alone. If you want to go far, go together'. Manifesting sustainable impact means mobilizing as one. Together.

The conundrum of love and fear has been with us as far back as we can see in history. The world's earliest recorded spiritual texts, the Vedas, c1500-500 BCE, captures a beautiful myth about the origins of love [106]:

> 'It all started with a superbeing called Purusha. This being had no desire, no craving, no fear, or indeed no impulse to do anything. Why? Well, the universe was already perfect and complete. The creator Brahma took his divine sword and split Purusha into two parts: separation and polarities emerged. Sky became separate from earth; darkness from light; life from death; and male from female. All the separated parts set off passionately to reunite with its counterpart. This process of seeking unity is the process of love.'

When we embrace the principle of unity, not only within a company but beyond a company, we can create 'man on the moon' experiences around a purpose, beyond money and glory.

When we as individuals and institutions dare to care for our customers and all our stakeholders, understanding that all they want is love and that we are dependent on them, we take our consciousness and mindset to another level.

When we dare to care about the community and the eco-system we are part of - as well as for the planet, our human and business transformation have the potential of becoming a social transformation, caring equally for all lives not only our own lives, including future generations. We unite beyond the boundaries of space and time.

As individuals and companies, we have a choice to make about whether we want to build an exploitative and degenerative culture or a nurturing, sustainable and regenerative company culture.

Regenerative means that we leave people, customers and other stakeholders better off with each interaction, engagement by engagement, conversation by conversation, intervention by intervention. When we consciously or unconsciously choose a win-lose approach, it is a degenerative approach where we waste capacity, impact, potential and life in general. We see so much waste produced in the world anchored in a mindset of fear.

At the same time there are so many pockets of hope and opportunity, anchored in a mindset of love, a regenerative mindset. For example, the world has never been safer with relatively few wars and the world is five percent greener now than it was two decades ago, with India and China leading the way in terms of tree planting [107].

The Ten Steps of Transformation demonstrate how we can choose deliberately to move from a fear-based vicious circle to a love-based virtuous circle. As we choose to step out of being paralyzed by the fear-driven cycle of separation, scarcity and the struggle for control and power, we begin to unfold the potential of a compassionate, empathic collaborative mindset, a culture of creativity and shared abundance for all. We move from a mindset of separation to unity and interbeing [108][109].

What impact are you manifesting in your life?

United in purpose, unique in perspective

Coming together as one is not the same as all being the same. We unite around one purpose for an organization bigger than ourselves and belong through our unique perspective and contribution to the bigger meaning.

When we observe how parts of the body collaborate when we breathe, we understand what we aspire to. Without capillaries we could not make that life sustaining exchange happen. Similarly, the life of a company cannot be sustained and enriched without its people. Often, we look at the top of the company to make transformation happen, whereas it belongs to all of us, and especially the mighty many – us, the people of the organization.

CEOs and senior executives are having shorter tenures in companies, often leaving or being asked to leave before the transformations are completed. A new CEO comes in and – way too often – starts a new journey, insufficiently building on the previous journey. What about all the people who put their hearts into the previous journey?

Every time the pendulum swings back and forth it leads to waste and value destruction. When we – the people of the organization – step in and take ownership for our own human transformation, enabling the business transformation, we create a more sustainable change. We create a win-win-win between the past, present and the future, as well as creating a win-win-win with our customers, partners and society.

As the mighty many, we are like the capillaries making the exchange happen, making the company breathe. Through the exchange with our surroundings we truly understand what makes the business flow, flourish and function. We make the business breathe – as we breathe business – where Transformational Capacity is not only built at the top – but in every one of us – enhancing the chances for success.

You might argue: 'If only I was the CEO, I would change my company.'

You are right. It is easier to influence a company from a position of a CEO ... and ... we have seen from history that single individuals can make a significant impact in the world – like Greta Thunberg championing for the climate alone in front of the Swedish parliament, on a Friday in August 2018.

Equally, you can make that happen in your company, impacting your surroundings with your positive ripple effect. You might not be the CEO of a company, but you are the perfect CEO of your life, including your work life, being the change would you like to see (Steps One-Ten). Your organization might be sizeable, and you might feel too insignificant for your endeavor. Research shows the tipping point for cultural change is only 25 percent, not 100 percent. When 25 percent of us are fully committed to changing behaviors and habits, new norms will be established. Through championing, conviction and commitment, the minority can become the majority! (110)

Embracing a loving mindset happens one person at a time and when enough people are moving mindsets in synchronicity, we are co-creating the culture of our company. In fact, we are our culture. Wherever we are, we will significantly and uniquely contribute when we embrace The Heart Revolution holding a mindset of love.

What do you know to be true?

I have come to learn that many words, including hope, try, believe, maybe, might, perhaps, probably, possibly, somewhat, kind of, sort of and really, are all fear-activated modifiers, distorting the truth. When my mind hesitates, I say 'I think', or 'I believe'. Meanwhile, my heart simply says 'I know'. I know love transforms lives. It transforms businesses.

What do you know to be true?

Always, if you are in doubt or want to accelerate your transformation, say to yourself what you know to be true: *'Everything I need is available to me, right here, right now.'*

We are highly privileged to be given the opportunity to live a life on this planet Earth. By learning, loving and living the mindset reflected in The Heart Revolution we are, together, able to give back what has been given to us.

Welcome to The Heart Revolution

An Action for All of Us

Dear Transformer

We are used to thinking about companies through the lens of levels and hierarchies, trying to manage people, rather than understanding each other as interlinked human beings. We tend to believe that we need to control and check on each other, rather than connecting and checking in with each other.

What can be seen as value in our local world might create waste for the totality – whereas, actually we are unique in our roles, our perspectives and our contributions and united in the purpose we are serving. When you learn to live with a loving mindset through this connected world-view, you are united in purpose, unique in perspective.

As an **individual,** the mighty many owning The Heart Revolution, you, through your daily practices build your Transformational Capacity, constantly and consciously choosing love before fear, allowing you to enjoy, grow and contribute significantly, in a fair exchange with your organization. When you are no longer able to serve your organization from a loving mindset, you know it is time for you to ask for help or to simply move on because you will never trade your integrity for convenience.

As a **leader,** owning The Heart Revolution, you know the journey starts with yourself and your ripple effect, creating learning environments where people can enjoy, grow and contribute. Securing your team bringing value to the totality; your company and beyond.

When you are no longer able to shine the light, supporting your people and serving your company by being a loving leader, you know it is time for you to step down or move on because you are no longer fulfilling the privileged role you are holding.

As an **executive,** owning The Heart Revolution, you courageously mobilize a regenerative culture, balancing and integrating the human and business transformation, paying equal attention to transforming and performing.

When you are no longer able to influence and stand by the direction set for the company, constantly integrating, avoiding the pendulum to swing too far to one side, you know that you are not serving your company. You choose to speak up, influence more, or leave your position as you need to be a brave and bold integrator.

As a **board member,** owning The Heart Revolution, you work to ensure the company creates balanced and fair value for all stakeholders.

When you are no longer able to focus on keeping the people in the company safe, but are more focused on keeping yourself and your board colleagues safe, you know it is time for you to change the dialogue in the boardroom, or step down from your role.

As a **business owner,** owning The Heart Revolution, you invest your money in companies providing sustainable and regenerative activities, serving your stakeholders, including future generations.

When the companies you have invested in are no longer making the world a better place, you know it is time for you to extract your money and invest in other initiatives that do.

As a **customer,** owning The Heart Revolution, you put your mouth and wallet where your values are, buying from companies doing well and doing good.

When you find yourself buying without thinking about whether you are harming future generations, you know you need to pause, connect and reflect.

Living in constant awareness, knowing that you have a choice moment by moment and acting with integrity to do what you truly believe in, is a constant journey. It starts with each one of us and only when we take full ownership for our choices and actions, will we manifest the impact we came here for.

Love

Acknowledgements

There are many people I want to honor for their contribution to this book; we are - together - many authors and creators of the insights and inspiration shared.

Emilie Bruun and **Mai Lynn Voldum,** have been amazing partners, holding the highest intention for this book all the way. Their knowledge, wisdom, experience, work capacity, as well as personalities are out of the extraordinary. We have loved and laughed much through the process.

The **Early** (beta) **Readers** of the manuscript have been exceptional providing feedback and new perspectives in a deeply caring way evolving and co-creating the book to what it is today.

Wendy Yorke has been a compassionate author coach. From the first day I met her, I knew we would click. A true joy.

Christian Mørk, the Danish author, has relentlessly pushed the boundaries for what was possible - helping to develop the book even further.

Lisa Doig, my coach and friend, has helped me during my transformational journey offering much wisdom, love, challenge, and support. In her capable hands, it is impossible not to stretch yourself, and so I did.

Michael, my life's partner, who supports me in all dimensions of life. He has been a critical and highly analytical voice in relation to the book and 'the work', always keeping me grounded. Without him this project and so many other things in my life would not have been possible.

My background

Born on a small farm in the Western part of Denmark, I grew up with animals and nature as my loved companions. My parents worked hard to make a living, providing for my two brothers and me. My home and family were full of energy, love and ambitions.

I loved school and as the hungry learner I am, I have kept studying for the majority of my life, following my passion: the intersection and sweet spot between human beings and businesses. Besides my initial education as a nurse, I hold a bachelor's degree in Economics specialized in Organizational Development; an Executive MBA; as well as a Master in Gestalt Psychotherapy.

As a nurse, I specialized in serving and caring for patients in critical conditions, supporting AIDS and intensive ward patients. Watching people dying with grace, gratitude and sometimes regrets, made me focused on never to take life for granted - devoting myself to supporting people and companies - to live their lives to the fullest.

The last 20 years, I have had a wonderful career holding executive roles, as well as board roles in global companies (30.000-115.000 people). In my leadership roles I have led teams in the intersection between people, organization, culture and communication - human and business transformations.

As a transformer, I have been privileged to design and deliver companywide transformations, working for market-leading companies in three different industries (software, technology and financial services) at a time when they have undergone massive disruptions. I have passionately facilitated the building of Transformational Capacity from the shop floor to the boardroom - always with the intention to inspire and equip people to take their place and find their path in the transformation, owning and leading it from the front.

With a desire to constantly raise the bar, I have focused on building an engaged workforce eager to turn business challenges, such as new technology, regulations and customer needs into opportunities. Most of all I have enjoyed the co-creation with the organization of new meaning and mindset; new company culture; new ways of leading and working; and engaging with customers and partners – manifesting impact through the integration and balance of human and business transformation.

Today, I have my own business advising organizations, teams and individuals to design and deliver business transformations, turning today's enormous waste of human capacity and business into value, by becoming purpose-led and values-driven human beings and businesses, which organizations, employees, customers and society can be proud of.

As an international speaker, I seek to disrupt and enrich my audience inviting them through love and laughter to step up their game in their private lives, as well as their businesses. I wish transformations not to be seen as scary, but as great opportunities for human beings and businesses to enhance their contribution, growth and enjoyment.

I have lived in several countries and worked across the globe. I am now enjoying living in Denmark with my partner Michael. Together, we explore nature by bike, wearing running shoes or a swimsuit; living a full life.

Notes

1. **Saint-Exupéry, Antoine de.** *The Little Prince.* s.l. : Mariner Books, 2000. ISBN13: 9780156012195.

2. **Hostrup, Hanne.** *Gestalt Therapy: An Introduction to the Basic Concepts of Gestalt Therapy.* s.l. : Museum Tusculanum Press, 2010. ISBN13: 9788763536578.

3. **Bucy, Michael, et al.** The 'how' of transformation. *mckinsey.com.* [Online] McKinsey & Company, Apr 2016. https://www.mckinsey.com/industries/retail/our-insights/the-how-of-transformation.

4. **Gallup.** *State of the Global Workplace.* s.l. : Gallup Inc., 2017.

5. **Jampolsky, Gerald G.** *Love Is Letting Go Of Fear.* s.l. : Celestial Arts, 2011. ISBN13: 9781587611186.

6. **Goleman, Daniel.** *Social Intelligence: The New Science of Human Relationships.* s.l. : Cornerstone, 2007. ISBN13: 9780099464921.

7. *The Prefrontal Cortex - An Update: Time Is of the Essence.* **Fuster, Joaquin M.** s.l. : Neuron, 2001, Vol. 30, pp. 319-333.

8. **HeartMath.** The Science of HeartMath. *heartmath.com.* [Online] HeartMath. https://www.heartmath.com/science/.

9. *The Role of Gratitude in Spiritual Well-being in Asymptomatic Heart Failure Patients.* **Mills, Paul J.** s.l. : Spirituality in Clinical Practice, 2015, Vol. 2. No 1, pp. 5-17.

10. **Barrett, Richard.** *The Values-Driven Organization: Unleashing Human Potential for Performance and Profit.* s.l. : Routledge, 2013. ISBN13: 9780415815031.

11. Stanford Medicine News Center. Positive attitude toward math predicts math achievement in kids. *www.med.stanford.edu.* [Online] Stanford Medicine, Jan 24, 2018. https://med.stanford.edu/news/all-news/2018/01/positive-attitude-toward-math-predicts-math-achievement-in-kids.html.

12. Achor, Shawn. *The Happiness Advantage - The Seven Principles of Positive Psychology That Fuel Success and Performance at Work.* s.l. : Crown Business, 2010. ISBN13: 9780307591548.

13. Mechlinski, Joe. Understanding The Three "Brains" in Our Body (And Their Critical Role at Work). *medium.com.* [Online] Medium, Sep 2018. https://medium.com/@joemechlinski_9502/understanding-the-three-brains-in-our-body-and-their-critical-role-at-work-d1715ae62bff.

14. Pillay, Srinivasan S. *Life Unlocked: 7 Revolutionary Lessons to Overcome Fear.* s.l. : Rodale Books, 2011. ISBN13: 9781609611460.

15. Scharmer, Otto and Kaeufer, Katrin. *Leading from the Emerging Future: From Ego-System to Eco-System Economies.* s.l. : Berrett-Koehler Publishers, 2013. ISBN13: 9781605099262.

16. Brown, Brené. *Daring Greatly - How the Courage to Be Vulnerable Transforms the Way We Live, Love, Parent, and Lead.* s.l. : Penguin Books Ltd, 2015. ISBN13: 9780241257401.

17. Schaninger, Bill and Keller, Scott. *Beyond Performance 2.0: A Proven Approach to Leading Large-Scale Change.* s.l. : Wiley, 2019. ISBN13: 9781119596653.

18. *Why Do So Many Managers Forget They're Human Beings?* **Hougaard, Rasmus, Carter, Jacqueline and Brewerton, Vince.** s.l. : Harward Business Review, Jan 29, 2018.

19. Hougaard, Rasmus and Carter, Jacqueline. *The Mind of the Leader: How to Lead Yourself, Your People, and Your Organization for Extraordinary Results.* s.l. : Harvard Business Review Press, 2018. ISBN13: 9781633693425.

20. Brandau, Karla and Ross, Douglas. *How to Earn the Gift of Discretionary Effort.* s.l. : Life Power Publishers, 2018. ISBN13: 9781892968111.

21. Sheth, Jagdish N. *Firms of Endearment: How World-Class Companies Profit from Passion and Purpose.* s.l. : Pearson Education (US), 2014. ISBN13: 9780133382594.

22. Linsky, Marty, et al. *The Practice of Adaptive Leadership.* s.l. : Harvard Business Review Press, 2009. ISBN13: 9781422105764.

23. Gandhi, Mahatma. *The Collected Works of Mahatma Gandhi (May-August 1924).* s.l. : Obscure Press, 2008. ISBN13: 9781443740203.

24. Ferrari, Pier Francesco and Rizzolatti, Giacomo. *New Frontiers in Mirror Neurons Research.* s.l. : Oxford University Press, 2015. ISBN13: 9780199686155.

25. Inspiring Leadership Now. 10 Of The Most Inspiring Leaders Of All Time: Remarkable Stories Of Iconic Trail Blazers Who Went From Adversity To Extraordinary & Redefined Leadership. *inspiringleadershipnow.com.* [Online] Aug 05, 2019. https://www.inspiringleadershipnow.com/ most-inspiring-leaders-redefine-leadership/.

26. Rumi. A Great Wagon. *Poem.*

27. *The Paradoxical Theory of Change.* **Beisser, Arnold.** s.l. : Gestalt Journal Press, 1970, Gestalt Therapy Now.

28. Goleman, Daniel. *Emotional Intelligence: Why it can matter more than IQ.* s.l. : Bloomsbury Publishing Plc, 1996. ISBN13: 9780747528302.

29. *Executive Control of Cognitive Processes in Task Switching.* **Rubinstein, Meyer and Evans.** 2001, Journal of Experimental Psychology: Human Perception and Performance, Vol. 27. No 4, pp. 763-797.

30. **Hougaard, Rasmus.** *One Second Ahead.* s.l. : Palgrave-Macmillan, 2015. ISBN13: 9781137551900.

31. **Campbell, Joseph.** *Pathways to Bliss – Mythology and Personal Transformation.* s.l. : New World Library, 2004. ISBN13: 9781577314714.

32. **Baumeister, Roy F.** *Meanings of Life.* s.l. : Guilford Publications, 1992. ISBN13: 9780898625318.

33. *Helping Your Team Feel the Purpose in Their Work.* **Cable, Dan.** s.l. : Harward Business Review, 2019.

34. **Hansen, Morten T.** *Great at Work: How Top Performers Do Less, Work Better, and Achieve More.* s.l. : Simon & Schuster, 2018. ISBN13: 9781476765624.

35. *The Benefits of Laughing in the Office.* **Heggie, Betty-Ann.** s.l. : Harward Business Review, Nov 16, 2018.

36. *A meta-analysis of positive humour in the workplace.* **Mesmer-Magnus, Jessica, Glew, David J. and Viswesvaran, Chockalingam.** s.l. : Journal of Manegerial Psychology, 2012, Vol. 27. No 2, pp. 155-190.

37. **Robinson, Lawrence, Smith, Melinda and Seagal, Jeanne.** Laughter is the Best Medicine. *Helpguide.org.* [Online] 2019. https://www.helpguide.org/articles/mental-health/laughter-is-the-best-medicine.htm?pdf=13511.

38. *The Journal of Henry David Thoreau.* **Thoreau, Henry David.** s.l. : The Walden Woods Project, Aug 5, 1851, Vol. II.

39. *Mind-Set Matters: Exercise and the Placebo Effect.* **Crum, Alia J. and Langer, Ellen J.** s.l. : Psychological Science, 2007, Vol. 18. No 2, pp. 165-171.

40. *Lottery Winners and Accident Victims: Is Happiness Relative?* **Brickman, Philip, Coates, Dan and Janoff-Bulman, Ronnie.** s.l. : Journal of Personality and Social Psychology, 1978, Vol. 36. No 8, pp. 917-927.

41. Perls, Frederick, Hefferline, Ralph F. and Goodman, Paul. *Gestalt Therapy: Excitement and Growth in the Human Personality.* s.l. : Souvenir Press Ltd, 1994. ISBN13: 9780285626652.

42. Dweck, Carol. *Mindset - Changing The Way You think To Fulfil Your Potential.* s.l. : Little, Brown Book Group, 2017. ISBN13: 9781472139955.

43. Frankl, Viktor E. *Man's Search For Meaning.* s.l. : Ebury Publishing, 2011. ISBN13: 9781846042843.

44. Abaci, Peter. *Conquer Your Chronic Pain: A Life-Changing Drug-Free Approach for Relief, Recovery, and Restoration.* s.l. : New Page Books, 2016. ISBN13: 9781632650528.

45. Revans, Reg. *ABC of Action Learning.* s.l. : Taylor & Francis Ltd, 2011. ISBN13: 9781409427032.

46. Famous Scientists. Alexander Fleming. *famousscientists.org.* [Online] Famous Scientists, 2009. https://www.famousscientists.org/alexander-fleming/.

47. Kipman, Sebastian. 15 Highly Successful People Who Failed On Their Way To Success. *lifehack.org.* [Online] Lifehack, 2019. https://www.lifehack.org/articles/productivity/15-highly-successful-people-who-failed-their-way-success.html.

48. **Robinson, Ryan.** How Steve Jobs Learned to Embrace Failure and Saved Apple. *www.thebalancesmb.com.* [Online] The Balance Small Business, 2019. https://www.thebalancesmb.com/steve-jobs-and-how-embracing-failure-saved-apple-1200640.

49. **Isaascon, Walter.** *Steve Jobs.* s.l. : Simon & Schuster, 2015. ISBN13: 9781501127625.

50. **Morgan, Jacob.** The Future of Education. *medium.com.* [Online] 2019. https://medium.com/@jacobm/the-future-of-education-b82bee273160.

51. **McKinsey Global Institute.** *Jobs Lost, Jobs Gained: Workforce Transitions in a time of Automation.* s.l. : McKinsey Global Institute, 2017.

52. **Petrie, Nick.** *Vertical Leadership Development - Part 1: Developing Leaders for a Complex World.* s.l. : Center for Creative Leadership.

53. —. *The How-To of Vertical Leadership Development - Part 2.* s.l. : Center for Creative Leadership.

54. **Anderson, Bob and Adams, Bill.** Reactive To Creative Leadership. *leadershipcircle.com.* [Online] https://leadershipcircle.com/wp-content/uploads/2019/01/Reactive-to-Creative-Leadership_edit.pdf.

55. **Gottman, John.** *Why Marriages Succeed or Fail - And How You Can Make Yours Last.* s.l. : Simon & Schuster, 1995. ISBN13: 9780684802411.

56. *How Toxic Colleagues Corrode Performance.* **Pearson, Christine and Porath, Christine.** s.l. : Harward Business Review, 2009.

57. *The Feedback Fallacy.* **Buckingham, Marcus and Goodall, Ashley.** Mar-Apr, s.l. : Harward Business Review, 2019.

58. Rosenthal, Robert and Jacobson, Lenore. *Pygmalion in the Classroom: Teacher Expectation and Pupil's Intellectual Development.* s.l. : Crown House Publishing, 2003. ISBN13: 9781904424062.

59. Brodherson, Marc, et al. Creativity's bottom line: How winning companies turn creativity into business value and growth. *mckinsey.com.* [Online] 2017. https://www.mckinsey.com/business-functions/mckinsey-digital/our-insights/creativitys-bottom-line-how-winning-companies-turn-creativity-into-business-value-and-growth.

60. Durant, Will. *The Story of Philosophy.* s.l. : Simon & Schuster, 1999. ISBN13: 9780671201593.

61. *There's a S.M.A.R.T. way to write management's goals and objectives.* **Doran, George T.** s.l. : Management Review, 1981, Vol. 70. No 11.

62. *How are habits formed: Modelling habit formation in the real world.* **Lally, Philippa, et al.** s.l. : European Journal of Social Psychology, 2010, Vol. 40, pp. 998-1009.

63. Goleman, Paul. *Change Your Habits, Change Your Life in 21 Days.* s.l. : CreateSpace Independent Publishing Platform, 2016. ISBN13: 9781533660183.

64. *The Making of a Corporate Athlete.* **Loehr, Jim and Schwartz, Tony.** s.l. : Harward Business Review, 2001.

65. Clear, James. *Atomic Habits: An Easy & Proven Way to Build Good Habits & Break Bad Ones.* s.l. : Penguin LCC US, 2018. ISBN13: 9780735211292.

66. Barker, Crawford and Hollingworth, Liz. How to use behavioural science to build new habits. *warc.com.* [Online] 2017. https://www.thebearchitects.com/assets/uploads/TBA_Warc_How_to_use_behavioural_science_to_build_habits.pdf.

67. Brewer, Judson. *The Craving Mind: From Cigarettes to Smartphones to Love – Why We Get Hooked and How We Can Break Bad Habits.* s.l. : Yale University Press, 2017. ISBN13: 9780300223248.

68. Oppong, Thomas. This is How to Increase The Odds of Reaching Your Goals by 95%. *medium.com.* [Online] Medium, 2017. https://medium.com/the-mission/the-accountability-effect-a-simple-way-to-achieve-your-goals-and-boost-your-performance-8a07c76ef53a.

69. Gladwell, Malcolm. *Outliers: The Story of Success.* s.l. : Little, Brown and Company, 2008. ISBN13: 9780316024976.

70. Byron, Katie and Williams, Carol. *Who Would You Be Without Your Story?* s.l. : Hay House Inc, 2008. ISBN13: 9781401921798.

71. University of Waterloo. Yoga and meditation improve brain function and energy levels. *www.medicalxpress.com.* [Online] Medical Xpress, Sep 06, 2017. https://medicalxpress.com/news/2017-09-yoga-meditation-brain-function-energy.html.

72. Keller, Scott and Schaninger, Bill. A better way to lead large-scale change. *www.mckinsey.com.* [Online] 2019. https://www.contextisleading.nl/wp-content/uploads/2019/08/A-better-way-to-lead-large-scale-change.pdf.

73. Smet, Aaron De, Schaninger, Bill and Smith, Matthew. The hidden value of organizational health – and how to capture it. *McKinsey Quarterley.* Apr, 2014.

74. Scharmer, Otto C. *Theory U: Leading from the Future as It Emerges.* s.l. : Berrett-koehler, 2016. ISBN13: 9781626567986.

75. Mintzberg, Henry. *Mintzberg on Management.* s.l. : Simon & Schuster, 2007. ISBN13: 9781416573197.

76. Katz, Daniel and Kahn, Robert L. *The Social Psychology of Organizations.* s.l. : Wiley, 1966. ISBN13: 9780471023555.

77. Aghina, Wouter, et al. The five trademarks of agile organizations. *www.mckinsey.com.* [Online] Jan 2018. https://www.mckinsey.com/business-functions/organization/our-insights/the-five-trademarks-of-agile-organizations.

78. Pawar, Manoj. Organizations As Living Systems: Lessons From Human Physiology. *The Systems Thinker.* Sep 2007, Vol. 18. No 7.

79. Chesterton, G. K. *Ultimate Collection: 200+ Novels, Historical Works, Theological Books, Essays, Short Stories, Plays & Poems.* s.l. : e-artnow, 2019. ISBN13: 9788027302062.

80. Yaffe, Philip. The 7% Rule: Fact, Fiction, or Misunderstanding. *Ubiquity.* Oct 2011.

81. *Listening, Hearing, Sensing: Three Modes of Being and the Phenomenology of Charles Sanders Peirce.* **Bodie, Graham D. and Crick, Nathan.** s.l. : International Communication Association, May 1, 2014, Communication Theory, Vol. 24. No 2, pp. 105-123.

82. Kenton, Will. The Triple Bottom Line (TBL). *www.investopedia.com.* [Online] Investopedia, May 03, 2019. https://www.investopedia.com/terms/t/triple-bottom-line.asp.

83. Fink, Larry. Larry Fink's Annual Letter to CEOs: A Sense of Purpose. *www.blackrock.com.* [Online] BlackRock, 2018. https://www.blackrock.com/hk/en/insights/larry-fink-ceo-letter.

84. Whittington, John. *Systemic Coaching and Constellations: The Principles, Practices and Application for Individuals, Teams and Groups.* s.l. : Kogan Page Ltd, 2016. ISBN13: 9780749475499.

85. **Heifetz, Ronald and Linsky, Marty.** *Leadership on the Line: Staying Alive Through the Dangers of Change.* s.l. : Harward Business Review Press, 2017. ISBN13: 9781633692831.

86. *The Power of Listening in Helping People Change.* **Itzchakov, Guy and Kluger, Avraham N. (Avi).** s.l. : Harward Business Rewiev, May 17, 2018.

87. **Mackey, John and Sisodia, Rai.** *Conscious Capitalism.* s.l. : Harward Business Review Press, 2013. ISBN13: 9781422144206.

88. **Senge, Peter and Scharmer, Otto C. et al.** *Presence - Exploring Profound Change in People, Organizations and Society.* s.l. : Nicholas Brealey Publishing, 2005. ISBN13: 9781857883558.

89. **Estrin, James.** https://lens.blogs.nytimes.com/. [Online] The New York Times, Aug 2015. https://lens.blogs.nytimes.com/2015/08/12/kodaks-first-digital-moment/.

90. **Djudjic, Dunja.** From Photo Industry Giant to Bankruptcy: What Happened to Kodak? *www.diyphotography.net.* [Online] DIYPhotography, Jun 2018. https://www.diyphotography.net/from-photo-industry-giant-to-bankruptcy-what-happened-to-kodak/.

91. **Birkinshaw, Julian and Brewis, Kathy.** Amazon: a master of reinvention. *www.london.edu.* [Online] Think at London Business School, Oct 12, 2016. https://www.london.edu/think/diie-innovation-icons-amazon.

92. **Repp, Kimberly.** How the Body Repair Itself. *www.askabiologist.asu.edu/.* [Online] Arizona State University. https://askabiologist.asu.edu/explore/when-body-attacked.

93. **Johnson, Barry.** *Polarity Management: Identifying and Managing Unsolvable Problems.* s.l. : Human Resource Development Press, 1996. ISBN13: 9780874251760.

94. **Steare, Roger.** The MoralDNA of Performance. *www.managers.org.uk.* [Online] Oct 2014. https://web.archive.org/web/20150518074353/http://www.managers.org.uk/~/media/Angela%20Media%20Library/pdfs/Research/The%20MoralDNA%20of%20Performance%20-%20October%202014.pdf.

95. *A Theory of Human Motivation.* **Maslow, A. H.** s.l. : Psychological Review, 1943, Vol. 50, pp. 370-396.

96. **Scott, Susan.** *Fierce Conversations - Achieving success in work and in life, one conversation at a time.* s.l. : Little, Brown Book Group, 2017. ISBN13: 9780349417363.

97. **Arens, Dan.** THE Characteristic Which Defines Leadership. *www.insideindianabusiness.com.* [Online] Inside INdiana Business With Gerry Dick, Nov 01, 2017. https://www.insideindianabusiness.com/story/36731269/the-characteristic-which-defines-leadership.

98. *The Emotions of Courage.* **Putman, Daniel.** s.l. : Journal of Social Philosophy, 2001, Vol. 32. No 4, pp. 463-474.

99. **SKYbrary.** B742 / B741, Tenerife Canary Islands Spain, 1977. *www.skybrary.aero.* [Online] SKYbrary, 1977. https://www.skybrary.aero/index.php/B742_/_B741,_Tenerife_Canary_Islands_Spain,_1977#.

100. **Edmondson, Amy C.** *The Fearless Organization: Creating Psychological Safety in the Workplace for Learning, Innovation, and Growth.* s.l. : John Wiley & Sons Inc, 2018. ISBN13: 9781119477242.

101. *The Creation of the Workplace Social Courage Scale (WSCS): An Investigation of Internal Consistency, Psychometric Properties, Validity, and Utility.* **Howard, Matt C., et al.** s.l. : Journal of Business and Psychology, 2017, Vol. 32, pp. 673-690.

102. **Porro, Cheryl.** Why I'm Setting Micro-Resolutions for a Mighty Impact. *thriveglobal.com.* [Online] Thrive Global, 2019. https://thriveglobal.com/stories/microstep-new-years-resolutions-stress-meditation/.

103. **Ware, Bronnie.** *The Top Five Regrets of the Dying: A Life Transformed by the Dearly Departing.* s.l. : Hay House, 2012. ISBN13: 9781401940652.

104. **Hawking, Stephen.** *Brief Answers to the Big Questions.* s.l. : Hodder And Stoughton Ltd., 2018. ISBN13: 9781473695986.

105. **Riley, Christopher.** Apollo 40 years on: how the moon missions changed the world for ever. *www.theguardian.com.* [Online] The Guardian, Dec 16, 2012. https://www.theguardian.com/science/2012/dec/16/apollo-legacy-moon-space-riley.

106. **Schiffman, Richard.** Ancient India's 5 Words for Love (And Why Knowing Them Can Heighten Your Happiness). *www.yesmagazine.org.* [Online] YES! MAGAZINE, Aug 14, 2014. https://www.yesmagazine.org/health-happiness/2014/08/14/ancient-india-s-five-words-for-love/.

107. **Tabor, Abby and Carlowicz, Mike.** China and India Lead the Way in Greening. *earthobservatory.nasa.gov.* [Online] NASA earth observatory, Feb 12, 2019. https://earthobservatory.nasa.gov/images/144540/china-and-india-lead-the-way-in-greening?src=ve.

108. **Wahl, Daniel Christian.** Why do we need to go beyond sustainability? *www.medium.com.* [Online] Goethe Institute Webinar 1. , Nov 29, 2019. https://medium.com/activate-the-future/why-we-need-to-go-beyond-sustainability-a869f8c16dc8.

109. **Wahl, Daniel Christian.** *Designing Regenerative Cultures.* s.l. : Triarchy Press, 2016. ISBN13: 9781909470774.

110. **Centola, Damon.** The 25 Percent Tipping Point for Social Change. *www.psychologytoday.com.* [Online] Psychology Today, May 28, 2019. https://www.psychologytoday.com/nz/blog/how-behavior-spreads/201905/the-25-percent-tipping-point-social-change.

Welcome to The Heart Revolution®

I'm so happy you've decided to commit to your transformation and have chosen to join The Heart Revolution!

Transformation is a continuous journey, so I'd love to stay connected with you, follow your personal journey, hear your ideas and insights, and have you join the digital Heart Revolution community.

Reach me directly:
karen.tobiasen@breathingbusiness.com

Stay connected and up-to-date on the latest transformation insights:

Karen Tobiasen: *karentobiasen.com*
YouTube: *youtube.karentobiasen.com*
Facebook: *facebook.karentobiasen.com*
LinkedIn: *linkedin.karentobiasen.com*

Explore how businesses can transform with Heart:
My company: *breathingbusiness.com*

Continue your growth in The School of Transformation®:

Enroll in the Transformational Capacity Program to deepen your understanding of the Ten Steps of Transformation and accelerate your journey.

Explore more: enroll.breathingbusiness.com

Karen is a business executive and transformer with 20+ years in People, Culture and Transformation leadership roles in several multinationals.

She has founded BreathingBusiness - a consultancy business that helps people and organizations to transform with heart.

Karen is a storyteller, collecting lightbulb moments when people do things, they never imagined was possible. She helps people and organizations through disruptive changes and guide people past fears and through transformations to enrich their professional and personal lives through love and laughter.

Most of all, she comes alive when she is deeply engaged in asking, listening to and sensing people - both what they're saying and not saying.

Karen is a lifelong student and learner, with a qualification as a nurse, a bachelor's in Economics, specialized in Organizational Development, anExecutive MBA and a Master's in Gestalt Psychotherapy.

Printed in Great Britain
by Amazon

47920146R00173